Cambridge Elements ☰

Elements in Politics and Society in Southeast Asia
edited by
Edward Aspinall
Australian National University
Meredith L. Weiss
University at Albany, SUNY

THE POLITICS OF RIGHTS AND SOUTHEAST ASIA

Lynette J. Chua
National University of Singapore

CAMBRIDGE
UNIVERSITY PRESS

University Printing House, Cambridge CB2 8BS, United Kingdom

One Liberty Plaza, 20th Floor, New York, NY 10006, USA

477 Williamstown Road, Port Melbourne, VIC 3207, Australia

314–321, 3rd Floor, Plot 3, Splendor Forum, Jasola District Centre,
New Delhi – 110025, India

103 Penang Road, #05–06/07, Visioncrest Commercial, Singapore 238467

Cambridge University Press is part of the University of Cambridge.

It furthers the University's mission by disseminating knowledge in the pursuit of
education, learning, and research at the highest international levels of excellence.

www.cambridge.org
Information on this title: www.cambridge.org/9781108719353
DOI: 10.1017/9781108750783

First published 2022

A catalogue record for this publication is available from the British Library.

ISBN 978-1-108-71935-3 Paperback
ISSN 2515-2998 (online)
ISSN 2515-298X (print)

The Politics of Rights and Southeast Asia

Elements in Politics and Society in Southeast Asia

DOI: 10.1017/9781108750783
First published online: May 2022

Lynette J. Chua
National University of Singapore

Author for correspondence: Lynette J. Chua, lynettechua@nus.edu.sg

Abstract: In this Element, I introduce the socio-legal study of politics of rights as the theoretical framework to understand rights in the culturally and politically diverse region of Southeast Asia. The politics of rights framework is empirically grounded and treats rights as social practices whereby rights' meanings and implications emerge from being put into action or mobilised. I elaborate on the concepts underlying politics of rights and develop an analysis of rights in Southeast Asia using this framework. The analysis focusses on: what are the structural conditions that influence the emergence of rights mobilisation? How do people mobilise rights and what forms does rights mobilisation take? What are the consequences of rights mobilisation and how do we assess them? I hope that this view of politics of rights - from a Global South region and from the ground - can encourage more astute evaluations of the power of rights.

Keywords: Rights, Resistance, Southeast Asia, Socio–legal Studies, Law and Society

ISBNs: 9781108719353 (PB), 9781108750783 (OC)
ISSNs: 2515-2998 (online), 2515-298X (print)

Contents

Introduction   1

1 Concepts and Features of Politics of Rights   7

2 Power and Control   14

3 Power and Resistance   23

4 Power of Rights   34

Conclusion   45

References   48

Introduction

How do we understand rights in regions comprising disparate cultures, societies and states, such as Southeast Asia? Three major challenges stand before anyone interested in rights in Southeast Asia: the diversity of the region, a sprawl of peninsulas and islands repeatedly divided and conquered by means of war and pillage, political conquests and legal fictions (Collier, Engel and Yngvesson 1994); the divergent interpretations, adaptations and uses of rights by actors with dissimilar positions and experiences; and, correspondingly, contrasting and often contradictory outcomes and evaluations of rights. Together, the three challenges convey an impression of messiness and incoherence as we survey the state of rights across Southeast Asia.

The first challenge, the region's diversity, stems from the numerous political, legal and social orders. Manifold normative orders, both official and non-official, shape the heterogenous ways in which Southeast Asians respond to their daily encounters and problems, understand themselves and relate to the state and others around them. This overall population of 650 million, who claim a mix of Indigenous and immigrant roots, live in cities, villages, highlands and forests demarcated by the borders of eleven sovereign nations whose political orders include democratic republic (Indonesia, Philippines, Singapore and Timor-Leste), constitutional monarchy (Cambodia, Malaysia and Thailand), absolute monarchy (Brunei), one-party communist state (Laos and Vietnam) and military dictatorship (Myanmar[1]). Among these eleven (see Figure 1), the larger states govern through several levels of administration, ranging from the federal down to the provincial, municipal and village levels. Each of the eleven states' political orders comes with its own legal order, which bears to varying degrees the imprints of pre-colonial kingdoms, sultanates and empires, followed by colonialism and post-colonial strife.[2] Each legal order of the state comprises constitutional law, statutory laws, court decisions and subsidiary legislation and regulations, as well as executive directives and policies; moreover, some of these legal orders apply different laws to certain subsets of the population within their jurisdictions. In addition, social orders, or non-state or non-official normative orders, co-exist with formal political and legal orders of the state. They include normative orders based in the world religions of

---

[1] After taking over an ostensibly democratic republic and proclaiming a year-long state of emergency on 1 February 2021, the Burmese military transferred government power to their commander-in-chief.

[2] The territories of contemporary Southeast Asian states have been colonized variably by the Portuguese, Dutch, French, British, Americans and Spanish. Only Thailand, previously known as Siam, was not formally colonised by Western powers.

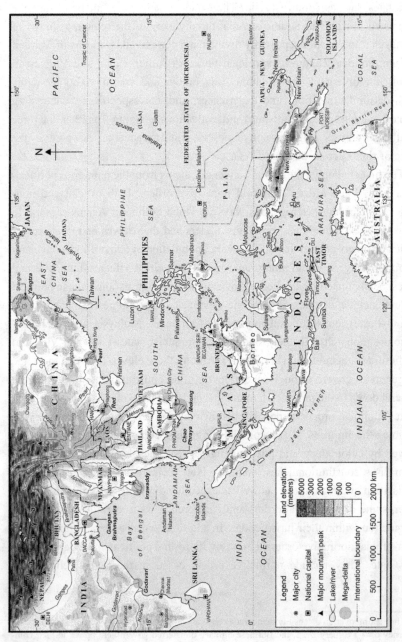

Figure 1 Map of Southeast Asia

Buddhism, Christianity, Hinduism and Islam; in local, animistic faiths; and in social groups such as clans and families.

The heterogenous official and non-official normative orders mould understandings of rights among Southeast Asians, such that one person's understandings would likely differ from those of the next. And, thus, the first challenge of studying rights in Southeast Asia corresponds to the second – the diverse interpretations, adaptations and usages of rights. What do Southeast Asians mean when they refer to rights? Rights have multiple genealogies in the region. Each of the eleven states has enacted its own bill of constitutional rights and an array of statutory rights. Some have also ratified international rights treaties: the Convention on the Elimination of All Forms of Discrimination against Women (CEDAW); the International Convention on the Elimination of All Forms of Racial Discrimination (ICERD); the Convention on the Rights of the Child (CRC); and the Convention on the Rights of Persons with Disabilities (CRPD).[3] Ten of the eleven states – Timor-Leste being the exception – belong to the regional body of the Association of Southeast Asian Nations (ASEAN), which has established human rights mechanisms in the form of the ASEAN Intergovernmental Commission on Human Rights (AICHR) and the ASEAN Human Rights Declaration (ADHR). Furthermore, United Nations agencies, non-governmental organisations (NGOs) and the embassies of Global North governments have disseminated international human rights discourse to Cambodia, Myanmar, Indonesia and other parts of Southeast Asia by implementing human rights programmes through state actors or providing funding and training directly to local populations.

Besides being traceable to diverse official sources, rights become even more complicated when Southeast Asians articulate their claims in languages of rights. The meanings and scope of rights put forth by claimants may differ from their formal definitions in domestic or international law. Even though claimants may pivot on official rights provisions for inspiration or legitimacy, they typically construct their distinctive understandings of rights with a richer collection of resources. They may draw not only from formal legal orders but also from social orders such as those related to religion, gender and family. In response, state actors and claimants' (other) opponents, who harbour their own preferred interpretations of rights, would fight to limit those of the claimants. As contestations and other interactions unfold among rights actors with divergent experiences and social positions, multiple interpretations, adaptations and applications of rights emerge and circulate.

---

[3] All eleven Southeast Asian states have ratified CEDAW and the CRC. Ten of these states, excluding Timor-Leste, are party to the CRPD, and nine of them, with the exception of Brunei and Malaysia, are party to ICERD.

Consequently, the third challenge is the plural and frequently inconsistent outcomes that flow from the diverse engagements with rights in Southeast Asia. In some instances, rights claimants triumph. They succeed at advocating for formal legislation that recognises their claims or win a court verdict in their favour. They persuade a government to enforce rights that protect a marginalised group from discrimination or to open up access to material resources to these populations. Furthermore, regional observers cautiously suggest that Southeast Asian states are growing receptive to and respectful of rights, pointing to evidence such as the ratification of international treaties, especially CEDAW, ICERD, the CRC and the CRPD, and the establishment of national human rights institutions (Duxbury and Tan 2019).[4] Nevertheless, in other instances, rights claimants lose. Their claims are rejected and their advocacy is crushed by the state or other powerful parties. They fail to move a wider audience or attract adequate support from intended allies. Going one step further, we could argue that Southeast Asia as a whole falls short of the aspirations of dignity, respect and equality that lie behind the bills of rights enshrined in domestic constitutions and international treaties. Human rights organisations regularly issue reports on the deliberate actions and neglect of Southeast Asian governments in fulfilling their rights obligations. Member states of ASEAN have also opted for enforcement mechanisms, the AICHR and the ADHR, that avoid direct intervention into the conduct of fellow members (Tan 2011), while member states like Myanmar actively carry out egregious rights violations.[5]

Because of the aforementioned challenges, studying rights in Southeast Asia requires an approach capable of giving due consideration to the region's complexities. In this Element, I introduce the socio-legal approach of 'politics of rights' as the analytical entry point.[6] According to this approach, rights are social practices whereby rights' meanings and implications emerge from their mobilisation – that is, from being put into action. To address frequently asked questions about rights, such as 'What do rights mean?', 'What can rights

---

[4] Among the eleven Southeast Asian states, Indonesia, Thailand, Malaysia, Myanmar, the Philippines and Timor-Leste have set up national human rights institutions to monitor and promote human rights in their respective countries. For a recent assessment of these six institutions, see Gomez and Ramcharan (2020).

[5] As a general principle, ASEAN member states do not intervene in the affairs of fellow members. However, following the Myanmar military's violent suppression of protests following the February 2021 coup, ASEAN made an unprecedented move in October 2021 to exclude the coup leader from a regional summit on the grounds that the military had failed to show any progress on a peace plan to which it had agreed with ASEAN earlier that year: www.bbc.com /news/world-asia-58938489 (last accessed 28 November 2021).

[6] There are, of course, theories on politics of rights in other fields, such as feminist studies (see, e.g., Zivi 2005; Cornwall and Molyneux 2008) and Foucauldian studies (see, e.g., Golder 2015).

accomplish?' and 'Can rights do any good for the weak and marginalised?', we examine real-life struggles over rights – how rights are asserted, applied, tested and contested. We collect and analyse empirical data – or pay attention to data analyses done by others – on the mobilisation of rights to formulate our answers to those questions. For the study of politics of rights, the answers do not lie in philosophy or abstract theorising nor in evaluating the correctness of statutes, constitutional documents, treaties or judicial opinions. If our research subjects argue that rights are naturally or divinely endowed, rely on official legal sources to support their arguments or bring up such 'cultural' postulations as 'Asian values', we treat those arguments, along with the fact that our research subjects employed them, as part of the data that we would examine.

The empirically informed nature of politics of rights makes it a highly suitable approach for studying rights in Southeast Asia and, by extension, other diverse societies and regions. Although its findings could lead to recommendations and critiques, the approach's primary aim is not to prescribe rights as a political solution nor to propose improvements to their application and contents – what I call the liberal rights perspective – nor is it to condemn rights as a neo-liberal, oppressive force acting against the governments and people of the Global South – what I describe as the critical rights perspective. In contrast to these two commonly held perspectives, the socio-legal politics of rights approach starts from the premise that we actually do not know much about rights among a certain population living in a specific context. So we first have to find out the 'how', 'what' and 'why', including but not limited to such issues as what the problem really is (rather than believing we know what the problem is); what the affected people know and think about rights; how they view rights as relevant or not relevant at all to the problem at hand; how they perceive and engage with rights; and what happens when they use rights to seek redress or recognition from powerful parties. Only after learning about the 'how', 'what' and 'why' are we then possibly in a better position to theorise about the potential and limits of rights and to formulate recommendations and criticisms.

I have organised the rest of this Element around key characteristics of politics of rights. In Section 1, I elaborate on the central concept of politics of rights, rights mobilisation, and the concept's three main features: decentring law on the books, interplay between structural and subjective conditions and plural practices of rights. These three features inform three important sets of inquiries in the socio-legal study of politics of rights, which I examine in the subsequent three sections: what are the structural conditions that influence the emergence of rights mobilisation (Section 2)? How do people mobilise rights and what forms does rights mobilisation take (Section 3)? What are the consequences of rights mobilisation and how do we assess them (Section 4)?

Related to the first set of inquiries – *What are the structural conditions that influence the emergence of rights mobilisation?* – I build on 'decentring law on the books' and 'interplay between structural and subjective conditions', the first two features of politics of rights, to elaborate on the existence of plural sites of power and domination in Southeast Asia – which is to say, the prevalence of authoritarianism at both state and non-state sites. The normative orders that hold together authoritarian sites of power manifest in the form of social controls, which range from the blatant to the elusive. Paying close attention to multiple and sometimes overlapping sites of authoritarianism and their social controls enables us to discern not only structural conditions that give rise to human suffering but also those conditions that shape the desire, ability and willingness to press for rights to change those circumstances.

However, it is not simply structural conditions that influence the prospects of rights mobilisation. Subjective conditions matter, too. Related to the second set of inquiries – *How do people mobilise rights and what forms does rights mobilisation take?* – I further highlight the feature of 'interplay between structural and subjective conditions', this time to show that rights mobilisation also depends on how people interpret their structural conditions and make decisions about what to do with them. Those who feel marginalised and decide to put up resistance by mobilising rights would do so in reaction to their specific conditions of authoritarianism and its particular modes of social controls. Hence, we find numerous practices of rights, the third feature of politics of rights. And we notice that Southeast Asians cumulatively produce a broad repertoire of rights practices that sit on three intersecting axes: uncoordinated to coordinated; covert to overt; and formal to non-formal.

The third set of inquiries – *What are the consequences of rights mobilisation and how do we assess them?* – pulls together all three features of politics of rights. Overall, the vast literature related to rights in Southeast Asia offers an untidy array of consequences: rights can vindicate the oppressed and empower the weak, but they can also disempower those who look to them for protection and fail to achieve their goals. Worse still, critical scholars opine, the decision to take up rights mobilisation, which may not result in successful outcomes, comes at the expense of alternative solutions, such as those rooted in more communitarian or local discourses, and the exacerbation of inequalities in Global South societies.

At the end of the Element, I ask that we give rights a chance, accepting the weight of their shortcomings while celebrating their lightness (McCann 2014). I return to the core of politics of rights, its premise that the meanings and effects of rights are empirically contingent and emerge from being claimed and contested. Structural conditions, which vary across time and place, matter to the development and trajectory of rights. So do the subjective conditions through which the weak encounter and face these structural odds, imagine what they can achieve and determine what they dare to carry out. It is my belief that the experiences of Southeast Asians – their heartaches, triumphs and struggles – can enhance the socio-legal study of politics of rights. And, thus, it is my hope that the view of politics of rights from below – from a Global South region and from the ground – can encourage more astute and careful evaluations of the power of rights.

1 Concepts and Features of Politics of Rights

Although the socio-legal study of politics of rights has roots in American-based research, over the past three decades scholars have enriched the field with research outside the United States, in societies ranging from liberal democracies to authoritarian regimes in Asia (see, e.g., Arrington and Goedde 2021; Wang and Liu 2020), Africa (see, e.g., Coulibaly, Claeys and Berson 2020; Morreira 2016;), Europe (see, e.g., Revillard 2017; Van der Vet 2018) and Latin America (see, e.g., Encarnación 2016; Speed 2008). Across these studies, rights mobilisation stands out as politics of rights' central operating concept.[7] Politics of rights is a social phenomenon that emerges from the processes of rights mobilisation, whereby rights claimants, their opponents and their supporters contend, collaborate or otherwise interact with one another.

Socio-legal scholars have defined rights mobilisation in a variety of ways. Synthesising foundational and influential texts in socio-legal research (see, e.g., McCann 1994; Scheingold 2004), I define rights mobilisation as social practices by which individuals or a group of people make sense of and express their problems in a language of rights. Co-labouring in groups or working individually, they interpret and adapt rights to fend off attacks, push back restrictions, recoup losses or fight for admission into institutions previously denied to them. They also use rights to empower others to participate in rights mobilisation.

As the main concept in politics of rights, rights mobilisation possesses three pertinent characteristics: the decentring of law on the books; interplay between structural and subjective conditions; and plural practices of rights. I have developed these features and their underlying theories based on my reading of

---

[7] In socio-legal literature, 'rights mobilisation' and 'legal mobilisation' tend to be conflated. For the most part, socio-legal scholars use the two concepts interchangeably. However, there may be situations in which the two concepts are not interchangeable – where law is mobilised without specific reference to rights (such as using a criminal provision to prosecute somebody) – and, in that sense, legal mobilisation is arguably the broader of the two.

politics of rights scholarship, my own research and a broad range of rights-related literature on Southeast Asian contexts.[8] I have also drawn upon the ideas of social theorists who have deeply influenced socio-legal studies to inform my own theorisation.[9]

1.1 Decentring Law on the Books

To decentre law on the books is to pay attention not only to official legal orders but also non-official normative orders when examining rights mobilisation. This feature does not suggest giving short shrift to or ignoring constitutional law, statutory legislation, court judgments, administration regulations and direct-ives, international rights conventions or other components of official legal orders when they are relevant to the case at hand. Rather, I highlight this feature to stress that we should not be immediately drawn to the pronouncements and conduct of formal institutions and their actors and proceed on the assumption that official laws define the scope and contents of any social phenomenon. It is important to find out and analyse whether there are other normative orders, beyond formal institutions, which also shape the issue, behaviours, thoughts and emotions involved.

Hence, 'decentring law on the books' distinguishes politics of rights from other approaches that scholars have engaged to study rights in the disciplines of law and international relations. By decentring law on the books, a bigger cast of actors fall within the scope of analysis. The principal cast would extend past lawyers, judges and other official legal actors to incorporate non-official or non-elite actors. To cite examples from Southeast Asian scholarship, the latter would include students (Weiss 2011), factory workers (Nguyen 2019), fishermen (Zerner 2003), peasants (Caouette and Turner 2009), migrants (Kemp and Kfir 2016) and refugees (McConnachie 2014). By comparison, jurists tend to privilege the opinions of state actors and formally trained legal experts when studying state obligations to uphold constitutional rights (see, e.g., Neo 2012), treaty provisions (see, e.g., Amirthalingam 2005) or court cases in domestic or transnational fora (see, e.g., Mohan 2013). To these scholars, formal articles of law and judicial opinions are authoritative pronouncements of what ought to be, with which they agree or disagree. Meanwhile, scholars who focus on inter-national relations or international law, such as ASEAN mechanisms (see, e.g., Eldridge 2002; Duxbury and Tan 2019) and national human rights institutions

---

[8] They include selections from socio-legal studies, geography, sociology, anthropology, politics, agrarian studies and history, just to name a few disciplines.

[9] These include, but are not limited to, Sewell (1992), Swidler (1986), Bourdieu (1977), Foucault (1979) and Gramsci (1971). My conceptualisation of power, therefore, contains features that span both structural accounts of power and post-structural, relational modes of power.

(see, e.g., Crouch 2013; Gomez and Ramcharan 2020), tend to concentrate on the extent to which governments have effectuated human rights and how they can do better. Their findings illuminate the reach of formal human rights law but reveal little about their impact on non-elites (Engel 2012). Although politics of rights scholars also want to understand formal actors, as a whole they are more likely to be interested in whether, how and why rights matter to ordinary folks as well.

Decentring law on the books is significant to all aspects of rights mobilisation, from emergence to the development of rights practices and to effects and outcomes. As we will see in detail in Section 2, authoritarianism resides in both state and non-state sites. It leads to human suffering or impede Southeast Asians from perceiving their grievous circumstances and identifying them as rights violations. It can assume the form of legal restrictions imposed by the state, such as curtailments on the activities of religious minorities or prohibitions on speech and assembly, as well as take on the form of non-official normative orders, such as societal standards governing women's conduct and company rules regulating female employees' dress and appearance. By tracing the impact of official laws and non-official orders, as we will notice in Section 3, different types of authoritarian powers and grievances push Southeast Asians to resist with a creative repertoire of rights practices. Some take to the streets against their governments (Engel 2016; Gillespie and Nguyen 2019), some pursue litigation to change formal laws (Moustafa 2018; Rosser 2015) and some write complaint letters to administrative agencies (Nguyen 2018). Additionally, away from the government and media spotlight there are those who quietly shore up grassroots support, recruiting and training new members for their cause (Chua 2019a; Nguyen 2019).

Finally, in line with decentring law on the books, when identifying and assessing the outcomes of rights mobilisation we should look for both instrumental and cultural effects. Instrumental effects correspond to law on the books, because they are usually the direct impact of rights mobilisation on official legal orders, like legislative reforms, court judgments or improved patterns of enforcement of official law. Cultural effects relate more closely to changes away from law on the books, like positive shifts to one's identity and self-efficacy and alterations to meanings, discourses and norms, which may reflect the indirect impact of official law or transformations of non-official normative orders. By going beyond the instrumental effects of rights and embracing its cultural effects, as we will see in Section 4, politics of rights expands the scope and ways in which we evaluate the consequences of rights mobilisation and thus the capacity of rights.

1.2 Interplay between Structural and Subjective Conditions

Rights mobilisation plays out through interactive processes between structural and subjective conditions, the heartbeat of politics of rights. 'Structural' refers to arrangements of people and their relationships at the macro level. Structural conditions possess normative force, which is often accompanied by sanctions and is capable of directing and patterning behaviour and ideas. The formal legal order of a state is a typical structure, a set of structural conditions comprising statutes, court judgments, regulations and enforcement procedures. A state's formal political order is another example of a structure consisting of rules on how to separate government into several branches, how to select and appoint office holders and so on. A bigger structure could include a formal political order and a non-official, often unwritten, normative order; the latter may contain such social norms as how politicians should behave and how dissenters should engage with them. Different structures, or sets of structural conditions, may overlap. Gender is usually a hybrid structure, composed of formal legal and political orders and non-official orders, regulating who counts as male or female and how different genders, such as men and women, ought to behave.

'Subjective' refers to perceptions, decisions, actions, thoughts and emotions at the micro level of individuals. Subjective conditions concern the manner in which people exercise agency: they construe and respond to structural conditions depending on who they are – for example, to which social groups they belong or are deemed by others to belong and their social position as a result of who they are. They also draw from their experiences accumulated from past interactions with structural conditions and other people. One person might wholeheartedly follow a particular normative order, such as laws that govern women's familial responsibilities; another person might challenge it, having considered alternative arrangements of gender roles set out in other normative orders, such as tribal customs or religion, or learned about women's rights from international NGOs. Such attention to subjective conditions should not be confused with the cultural relativism of 'Asian values' arguments, which Southeast Asian politicians the likes of Mahathir Mohamad and Lee Kuan Yew have championed (Bell 2000). Whereas 'Asian values' proponents take a prescriptive position towards rights, typically arguing that they are incompatible with local 'culture', politics of rights scholars treat subjective conditions as data with which to analyse human agency in relation to a given set of structural conditions.

Subjective responses to structures make up social practices. Assuming the forms of actions, words, thoughts and emotions, social practices can give life to structures or weaken them. Structures do not possess normative and sanctioning force by their mere presence. They are real only if they continue to exert authority and influence by being constantly put into action. A formal legal order truly exists as a structure when state actors enforce its laws and citizens follow or even believe in them, by engaging in practices such as social controls, which we will discuss in detail in Section 2. Conversely, structures fall into disuse and lose authority if interplays between the structural and subjective increasingly produce resistance-oriented practices, such as rights practices, which deviate from or oppose these existing structural conditions.

Each social practice comprises a distinctive assembly of tangible and intangible resources (Sewell 1992) – such as information, human connections and money – linked to existing structures and also possibly to practices that have started to circulate but have not necessarily helped to establish any structure at a given site. Having reconsidered their decisions or acquired new resources, people can innovate social practices and adopt resistant ones by putting together resources differently. If more and more engage with novel practices and keep them in use, new structures could emerge. Therefore, rights practices can eventually institute a new structure of rights.[10] In Myanmar, Cambodia, Laos and many more societies and communities in Southeast Asia, there is probably no durable rights structure in place, though we can find related resources in existing legal orders, such as a constitutional bill of rights, that are not given much force in reality. However, it is possible for residents in these societies to rearrange resources and generate fresh responses, including rights practices, which we will discuss in Section 3.

Interplays between the structural and subjective remind us that structural conditions do not necessarily determine the emergence nor development of rights mobilisation. Subjective conditions, how people exercise agency in relation to the former, matter as well. In face of harsh structural conditions, some may resign themselves to their circumstances, while others may resist and may turn to rights as one of their options. That is why in Southeast Asia, time after time, local populations have risen up in defiance of dangerous and hostile conditions. Among the memorable uprisings in recent history are the 1988, 2008 and 2021 protests in Myanmar against military rule; the 1988 People Power Movement against the Marcos regime of the Philippines; and the 1973 and 2020–1 protests in Thailand against military dictatorship and the monarchy, respectively.

1.3 Plural Practices of Rights

Decentring law on the books and the interplay between subjective and structural conditions lead us to the third feature of rights mobilisation, the

---

[10] On rights as structure, see the discussion of emic and etic sensibilities in Section 1.3 and of rights hegemony in Section 4.3.

plurality of rights practices. Especially in a diverse region like Southeast Asia, people living with different subjective or structural conditions, or both, are going to enact disparate social practices as they tap resources unevenly and unequally available to them. Thus, rights mobilisation is usually contentious. The rights practices of mobilisers may suffer rebuke from state actors or encounter animosity from other opponents. These other actors may reject rights claims altogether or prefer to practise their own version of rights to the exclusion of mobilisers' claims. With new interactions and experiences, mobilisers may go on to adjust and modify their rights practices, and the interplays of the subjective and structural continue to unfold.

The plurality of rights practices indicates that rights, conceptualised as social practices in the study of politics of rights, are malleable and contingent. At this juncture, we arrive at a crucial quandary that has lain embedded in politics of rights scholarship but has been usually left unaddressed. If the weak and marginalised can adapt and (re-)invent the meanings of rights, so can the elite and powerful. The latter, too, can mobilise rights to preserve privileges and benefits that exclude the former, strengthen structural conditions that favour themselves or even insidiously influence subjective conditions of the weak to reduce opposition and resistance. Moreover, since rights are meant to prevent or mandate certain behaviour, the elite and powerful might also oppose the rights claims of marginalised groups on the grounds that recognising those claims would cause them to suffer under authoritarianism. Of course, the elite and powerful might not declare their oppressive intention and might even claim to be motivated by justice or to defend from a position of inferiority. In socio-legal studies, scholars have analysed the phenomena of rights mobilisation by politically powerful conservative groups (see, e.g., Dudas 2008; Lehoucq 2021). However, because politics of rights – with its roots in the American civil rights movement (Scheingold 2004) – is usually concerned with progressive justice for disenfranchised or dispossessed populations, the malleability of rights as social practice leads to a thorny predicament. How should we treat the mobilisation of rights by the elite and powerful?

To get out of this quandary, I would suggest applying the politics of rights framework with both emic and etic sensibilities: when explaining how people mobilise rights, we would take an emic approach to examine the subjective conditions of mobilisers, regardless of their motives and social positions, and understand from the mobilisers' perspectives their thoughts, actions and feelings. When explaining the significance of our research findings, we would adopt an etic approach to analyse the structural conditions, tactics and their consequences from our own perspectives as scholars, what we consider to be significant to our academic field.[11]

Based on etic assessment, we would consider as resisters people who mobilise from or on behalf of those in positions of subordination vis-à-vis their superordinates to challenge inequality, exploitation or oppression (Fletcher 2007). Therefore, in Southeast Asia, resisters would likely include ethnic minorities, religious minorities, women, sexual and gender minorities, the impoverished, the unpropertied and others who are disenfranchised or dispossessed, as well as activists who advocate for such populations. Importantly, we would discern whether their intentions are to oppose a superordinate's authority and dispute their power and privileges – in which case the intentions would be resistant – or simply to reap personal benefit or to undercut or profit at the expense of others in similarly subordinated positions (Kerkvliet 2009). For example, when a group of Western Penan in Sarawak confronted timber companies, they did so out of unhappiness that they had received less compensation than other Western Penan groups (Brosius 1997). Although it was the timber companies' destruction of their ancestral lands that triggered the quarrel over compensation, these Western Penan were motivated to get ahead of intra-tribal rivals. Therefore, exercising our etic discretion, we would not regard them as having acted in resistance.

As for those who mobilise rights to maintain their superior position over other individuals and groups and keep their exclusive privileges and benefits, we would label them as anti-resisters. For instance, in the 2010s, extremist group Ma Ba Tha advocated for the rights of the overwhelming majority in Myanmar, Bamar Buddhists, lobbying for restrictions on Muslim minorities' freedom to marry and bear children (Walton, McKay and Daw Khin Mar Mar Kyi 2015); Vietnamese capitalist, upper-class farmers campaigned to win back their land rights in the late 1980s, resulting in the displacement of thousands of rural poor who had received land for subsistence agriculture under the government's redistribution programme (Gorman 2014). As scholars, we would be interested in the rights mobilisation of the likes of Ma Ba Tha and Vietnamese upper-class farmers. However, we would not treat such advocates and campaigners as oppressed parties but as the opponents of resisters who want to improve their structural conditions.[12] Similarly, we would apply the same emic/etic strategy to

---

[11] For a recent and general summary of emic and etic approaches, see Mostowlansky and Rota (2020).

[12] A related challenge concerns language. Especially in a linguistically and culturally diverse region like Southeast Asia, in the process of interpretation and adaptation rights might not be communicated or even imagined in the English language. It is also possible that there is no easy or direct translation of the word 'rights' from English. For example, Myanmar activists often translate 'rights' as 'akwint ayay', but that word literally refers to concepts such as

deal with the contention that recognising the rights of marginalised claimants would result in the oppression of anti-resisters, who occupy elite and powerful positions. We would call upon our emic sensibilities to study how a group of people subjectively experience the impact of rights. Then we would switch over to our etic sensibilities to consider whether they are actually the beneficiaries of the authoritarianism at which resisters' claims were directed and whether these anti-resisters now refuse to accept the changes aimed at improving the conditions of resisters.

The three features of rights mobilisation take centre stage in the next three sections. First, decentring law on the books and the interplay between subjective and structural conditions open up our examination of structural conditions that shape the emergence of rights mobilisation in Southeast Asia. Second, the interplay between the structural and subjective and the existence of plural rights practices illuminate the broad array of rights practices by Southeast Asians. Third, we come full circle and round up all three features to consider how we can assess the effectiveness of rights through the lenses of politics of rights.

2 Power and Control

No matter how desperate they feel, the weak and marginalised do not always challenge their grievous circumstances and, if they do, they do not necessarily resort to rights. If human misery were an adequate condition for spurring rights claims, there would be many more episodes of mobilisation and much more urgency.[13] Therefore, as we view Southeast Asia through the analytical framework of politics of rights, we should begin with the emergence of rights mobilisation and the structural conditions that it goes up against.

To examine the impact of structural conditions, we first need to locate what I call sites of authoritarianism or authoritarian power. Additionally, we need to recognise how authoritarianism exerts itself through social practices known as social controls, which operate in modes ranging from the overt to the elusive.

'opportunities' and does not exactly mean 'rights' (Keeler 2017). How do we know rights mobilisers are talking about rights? Again, I would propose the emic/etic approach. From an emic standpoint, we would ask whether they are articulating their own rights language in a way that completely mirrors the original word in their native language (such as 'opportunities' in the Myanmar example) or whether they have given the word a different connotation. After that, we would toggle over to etic sensibilities to analyse whether their version of rights possesses characteristics that signal resistance – for instance, whether they are deploying rights against inequality, exploitation or oppression or are advocating for their 'rights' in order to put down, exclude or harm other groups intentionally.

[13] Generally, social movements studies point out that miserable human conditions are insufficient to set off collective action (see, e.g., McAdam 1999).

Understanding where and how authoritarianism manifests enables us to better analyse the conditions under which rights mobilisation may or may not emerge. Thus, the question for this section – *What are the structural conditions that influence the emergence of rights mobilisation?* – relates to the first feature of rights mobilisation, the decentring of law on the books, and to the second feature, the interplay between structural and subjective conditions.

2.1 Plural Sites of Authoritarianism

When we think of authoritarianism, we usually come up with a list of states. Laos, Vietnam, Myanmar and a few others in Southeast Asia would probably appear on that list. However, the state is not the only site of authoritarian power. Building on the rights mobilisation feature of decentring law on the books, we open up our horizons to many more sites of authoritarianism, both state and non-state. Southeast Asia aptly illustrates this all-over nature of authoritarianism. In the Introduction, I offered a long but non-exhaustive list of official and non-official normative orders in the region, any one of which can constitute an authoritarian site.

Instead of primarily associating authoritarianism with states and their formal structures, in an earlier article (Chua 2019b) I asked socio-legal scholars to focus on the essence of authoritarianism, which is power that perpetuates the domination of an individual or group over social relations and protects the dominant individual or group's accompanying privileges and interests. Hence, authoritarianism emanates from and resides within multiple sites, a perspective that resonates with classic socio-legal texts (see, e.g., Fraenkel 1941; Nonet and Selznick 1978) and theories in the broader social sciences (see, e.g., Armstrong and Bernstein 2008; Fligstein and McAdam 2011). Authoritarian sites include formal state apparatuses, religious communities, tribes, political parties, corporations, gangs, social clubs, clans and families. Each site consists of one or more normative orders that make up structures, setting out rules to govern and sanction conduct, as well as possibly thoughts and feelings. Moreover, each site may overlap with other sites to generate interrelated effects of authoritarianism.

One might object that such a notion of authoritarianism would expand the presence of authoritarianism to anywhere and everywhere. But why not? Doing so openly admits that most people in Southeast Asia and elsewhere around the world live under some type of domination and subjugation. This perspective acknowledges that authoritarianism is not an exception but a common phenomenon; domination by formal state institutions and control of social relations by non-state orders exist along a continuum, whose differences are a matter of degree and shape. Moreover, this 'all-over' perspective does not suggest that authoritarianism works in similar fashion everywhere. Scholars already argue that the line between democracies and non-democracies is blurry and that the two appear at polar ends of a sliding scale (Varol 2015). Similarly, authoritarianism can assume different guises and degrees of influence.

At state sites of authoritarianism, interdependent structures such as legal and political orders may produce layers of authoritarianism with varying coverage. Some layers spread across nationwide structures. Others are confined to subnational territories, such as shariah legal orders at the level of Malaysia's federated states. Still others constitute enclaves within state structures to target specific individuals or groups. Malaysia's *bumiputera* policy that gives preferential treatment to the Malay majority in public service, public education, property, business and other sectors (Kananatu 2020); Thailand's discriminatory management of non-ethnic Thai highlanders (Hall, Hirsch and Li 2011); and Myanmar's violent exclusion of ethnic minorities (Cheesman 2017) are examples reminiscent of racist authoritarian enclaves in apartheid South Africa and the southern states of the United States (Smith 1997).

Non-state sites of authoritarianism can operate in collaboration or cooperation with the state's. Across Southeast Asia – such as in factories in Vietnam (Nguyen 2019), refugee camps along the Thailand–Myanmar border (McConnachie 2014) and construction sites in Singapore (Bal 2015), just to name a few – the poor and underclass have less recourse to state protection than the affluent, the ethnic majority or those whom the state deems to be citizens. Conversely, non-state sites of authoritarianism can also counteract state legal orders, which may, in fact, provide relief or protection to the weak. Kent (2011), for example, learned that Cambodian women in her study did not want to vindicate their rights through state courts against their attackers but sought 'moral rehabilitation' in Buddhist temples, which, in my view, can be regarded as non-state sites of authoritarianism. These temples enforce a patriarchal order according to which women, by virtue of being born female, are considered inferior to men, treated as too impure (due to menstruation) to come into direct contact with monks and implored not to hold their male attackers accountable but to attribute their experiences of sexual assault to bad karma accumulated from their own transgressions in previous lives.

2.2 Social Controls

As I pointed out in Section 1, 'Concepts and Features of Politics of Rights', structures have to be constantly practised to continue possessing normative and sanctioning force. By extension, so do structures whose normative orders compose authoritarianism. Interplays between structural and subjective conditions that enact practices known as social controls give effect to authoritarianism, if and when state actors enforce these social controls or when individuals or groups of people obey or even support them. In other words, whereas rights mobilisation are social practices that resist authoritarianism, social controls realise and enliven authoritarianism.

Social controls safeguard the status, privileges and interests of dominant groups and individuals at their given sites of authoritarian power by imposing and extracting conformity to a certain morality, economic production or political hierarchy. Social controls that regulate morality prescribe 'correct' ways of life and attempt to alienate or eliminate alternatives. For example, in Southeast Asia, patriarchal societies and communities circumscribe the conduct and mobility of women (see, e.g., Atsufumi 2016; Harriden 2012); and governments that adopt a state religion try to homogenise the practices of that religion (see, e.g., Hamid 2016) and restrict the activities of other faiths (see, e.g., Hayward and Frydenlund 2019). Controls that regulate economic production aim at ensuring those in power – such as wealthy landlords and governments – can quantify, assess and tax their targeted populations' economic output (Scott 2009). Controls that keep the less powerful, usually women and minorities, in their places aim to maximise and maintain the political advantage of the dominant, thus also securing their moral and economic superiority. Complementing or emboldening one another, moral, economic and political controls target the material, such as financial and natural resources, employment and housing; or the cultural, such as identity, ideas and discourses. The result is the limitation or erosion of de jure or de facto rights that provide entitlements, benefits, protection or status to marginalised populations, violence and differential treatments against these populations or inertia when such acts are perpetrated by others.

Social controls vary in their degree of explicitness and manner of extracting conformity, ranging from being obvious to imperceptible and from the extraordinary to the routine. They can appear as physical things, such as barriers, weapons and handcuffs; in written or spoken language, such as legal restrictions and threats; in the form of actions, such as killing, prosecuting or shouting; and in the shape of ideas and discourses, the way we think and feel – or rather, how we believe how we ought to think and feel. At first glance, the things that count as structures and those that count as practices, social controls, seem to overlap. For example, when I referred to laws making up an authoritarian legal order, I appear to have classified them as social controls, too. However, the linchpin is social practice. A restrictive law that forms part of an authoritarian legal order manifests as a social control if the state actually deploys it to prosecute dissenters or if dissenters perceive it to be a threat and deter their behaviour as a consequence. If the same law is left dormant on the books, unenforced or absent from the minds of people, such that it has no real-life implication, it would not amount to being a social control.

Based on my survey of Southeast Asian-based research and socio-legal studies at large, we can organise social controls into three modes along a spectrum. At one end we find the most blatant and most easily detectable (overt) social controls. As we move towards the middle, we locate less overt but still somewhat obvious modes. Then, as we travel from the middle to the other end of the spectrum, we encounter increasingly elusive modes of control. Obvious modes of controls include patent violence, intimidations and extra-legal and illegal measures. Somewhat less obvious modes offer limited opportunities for dissent and redress but without ceding the status quo. Elusive modes regulate information, discourse and action, and the most imperceptible ones can even normalise preferred ideologies and behaviour. We can probably discern the state or non-state authoritarian, such as a patriarch, religious leader or corporation, wielding an obvious mode of control. As the controls grow more elusive, we may not be able to do so easily. The subtler the control, the less likely we can pinpoint the individual, group or entity behind it. Nevertheless, the dominant parties or those in power remain the beneficiaries, if not masters, of such controls.

Readers might not entirely agree with my placements of certain controls along the spectrum. This is to be expected, and it is why I plot social controls along a spectrum rather than categorically name them as overt or elusive. A social control can manifest in more than one mode of perceptibility and imperceptibility. A law that bans street demonstrations (obvious mode) could also channel dissent (Earl 2011) into venues that are acceptable to the authoritarians in charge (less obvious mode), for example by allowing public gatherings only at a designated location. Additionally, this law could discipline subjects so that they come to believe in the impropriety of such actions as street demonstrations (more elusive mode). Furthermore, one mode of control reinforces another in back and forth directions. In the same example on street demonstrations, stepping out of the legally permissible channel to air dissent could trigger explicit sanctions of arrest and expulsion. Together, the different modes of controls, from the obvious to the subtle, could add up and impede the prospects of rights mobilisation.[14]

2.2.1 Overt Modes

Social controls clustered at the overt end of the continuum are obvious in the sense that the populations singled out for control are cognisant of these controls. Whether or not they contravene them, they are aware that these controls are

---

[14] My elucidation of social controls is informed by Digeser (1992), Gaventa (1982), Lukes (1974) and Schattschneider (1975).

meant to prevent and dictate their conduct. They are also aware of the consequences if they were to violate the controls.

The most recognisable types of overt controls are likely outright violence and intimidations of violence. They include incidents of physical harm, death, capture and detention that attempt to coerce people into keeping quiet about their troubles or stop them from seeking any remedy. In Southeast Asia, scholars have documented extra-legal and illegal force by state actors and extremist groups such as the Khmer Rouge's mass murders (see, e.g., Gidley 2019; Manning 2017) and the torture, assassinations and disappearances by the governments of Thailand (see, e.g., Haberkorn 2018), Laos (see, e.g., Sims 2020) and Myanmar (see, e.g., Cheesman 2016). Even when recourse to state law is available, the silenced dissenter may be unable or unwilling to press charges against mega-corporations, the government and other powerful parties for fear of repercussions. Time and again, scholars have exposed the abuse of power, corruption and executive intimidation of Southeast Asian judiciaries, including Myanmar's (Cheesman 2015) and Timor-Leste's (Grenfell 2015; Jeffrey 2016).

Besides blatant and bloody violence, repressive laws (Nonet and Selznick 1978) can also control dissent. For instance, Indonesia and Cambodia in recent years have passed laws on freedom of association, respectively, to curb the expansion of social movements (Caraway and Ford 2020) and non-governmental organisations (Curley 2018). As Rajah (2012) wrote in her Singaporean study, laws can be used as a weapon to achieve authoritarian rule while appearing to uphold 'rule of law'; or, in Cheesman's words from his study of colonial and post-colonial Burmese governments, law can be weaponised to stifle claims for rights and democracy in the name of 'law and order' (2015). Arrest, detention, prosecution, fines and imprisonment – the consequences of legal violation – can reduce dissenters' ability to speak out, harm their sense of security and livelihood or deplete their financial resources. Furthermore, as Yew (2016) documented in his study of environmental rights activism in Malaysia, the existence of such laws and mere inklings of their enforcement, usually in the form of surveillance, could be enough to deter mobilisation. Although the proliferation of Internet access and social media has opened up alternatives and opportunities to circumvent restrictions on speech and assembly (Weiss 2012), Southeast Asian governments have also caught up with technological advancements and expanded their curtailments on speech and expression to new media (Weiss 2014).

At non-state sites of authoritarianism, there are also social controls of explicit force and proscription. In my study of lesbian rights activism in Myanmar (Chua 2016), for example, I found that women enjoyed less freedom to participate in meetings, demonstrations, trainings and other movement activities, because their elder brothers, uncles or fathers forbade them from going out at certain times, especially at night. According to Nguyen's (2019) ethnographic study of labour rights activism in Vietnam, factory workers refused to file formal complaints or lawsuits against employers who had violated their legally entitled rights in state law, because they feared retaliative acts of dismissal or demotion. For similar reasons, scholars conducting research in Thailand (Christensen and Rabibhadana 1994), Philippines (Silliman 1981–2), Myanmar (Cheesman and Kyaw Min San 2013) and Indonesia (Aspinall 2013) find that the lower classes in those societies were often reluctant to assert their rights against wealthy individuals or officials for fear that they would court more trouble in return.

2.2.2 Somewhat Overt and Elusive

Social controls around the central region of the spectrum are less overt but not entirely invisible – they are more discreet but still discernible. Unlike outright attacks and bans, controls in this part of the spectrum seem innocuous, neutral or even helpful to marginalised individuals and groups. The targeted population might enjoy some leeway to express their dissatisfaction and make demands. At the same time, this type of social control prescribes and limits their expressions and demands so that they do not fundamentally threaten the status quo, which is why scholars have described such controls as agenda setting (Kessler 1990) or channelling (Earl 2011).

The same laws and restrictions at the overt end of the spectrum could resurface here as being somewhat overt and elusive. Take for instance state laws that restrict the freedom of association in Singapore, requiring groups exceeding a certain size to register with the government. Alongside the overt mode of social control – criminal sanction – a channelling effect could be taking place more subtly. By complying with the state's registration requirements, activists cannot freely raise funds and have to exercise further caution when advocating for political rights (Chua and Hildebrandt 2014). Over time, their limited scope of mobilisation could cumulatively diminish the force of civil society (Rodan 2003). Court rules on standing and leave, which determine whose lawsuits can be heard, are another example. Due to conservative court rules in Singapore, activists cannot directly litigate for the rights of migrant workers (Kemp and Kfir 2016), and thus the delicate issues of migrant rights and labour rights are excluded from the courts by a neutral-looking procedural law. Yet other examples involve definitions that bestow recognition upon certain populations or organise certain claims out of the terms of discussion.

Thus, anthropologists noted, by formalising property ownership of forest land, the Indonesian state ended up illegitimising Indigenous populations' customary entitlements to natural resources (Peluso 2003; Zerner 2003); in Myanmar, by classifying populations into 'official' ethnicities and 'national races', terminologies that exclude the Rohingya, successive post-colonial governments have predetermined the outcome of Rohingya claims to citizenship rights (Cheesman 2017).

At Southeast Asia's regional level, we can also identify semi-elusive controls. Arguably, ASEAN principles of consultation, consensus and non-intervention embody an agenda-setting effect. Even though the principles signal ASEAN members' respect for one another's sovereignty in light of their histories of colonialism and foreign intervention, adherence to the principles could result in impunity for actions such as the persecution of ethnic minorities and the maltreatment of refugees within a member state's borders. Moreover, ASEAN members set the agenda by taking contentious issues off the table when they put up reservations to the ADHR to relieve themselves of obligations such as the assurance of equality for Muslim women in matters of marriage and inheritance (Duxbury and Tan 2019). The lack of an adjudication forum for individual citizens to sue their governments directly under the ADHR (Duxbury and Tan 2019), too, organises away grievances from ASEAN's purview.

2.2.3 Elusive Modes

As we approach the other end of the spectrum, social controls grow increasingly subtle and indiscernible. Unlike when they experience the modes of controls on other parts of the spectrum, the subordinated may not even realise that they are under the influence of elusive controls. They may not even perceive that they have suffered a wrong and may not regard their experiences as problematic or relevant to rights, such that rights mobilisation is not a consideration at all. The less obvious the control and the closer it lies towards this end of the spectrum, the less cognisant the subordinated may be of its presence and effects. These controls could make certain ways of life feel normal or natural by shaping wants, interests and meanings of relationships and self or by disciplining actions and thoughts. If enough people succumb to 'inner feelings of guilt' (Nonet and Selznick 1978, pp. 49–50), eventually the authoritarian's preferred ideas, actions and ways of life might no longer be questioned and become accepted as normal. In the worst-case scenario, the subordinated might even actively enforce the social control against others similarly subordinated (Ibrahim 2018).

The restrictions and measures that exert explicit and overt modes of control, which we discussed earlier, are connected to elusive modes at this end of the spectrum as well. Physical violence, stringent laws and their threats, and surveillance could lead to the effect of limiting access to information about rights, since fewer would dare to look for the information, openly advocate for rights or reach out to others to engage in rights mobilisation. Over time, rights may fade away from imaginations of the possible. Hence, Burmese activists in my study, who grew up under military dictatorship in the 1980s and 1990s and had little access to information about rights, used to associate rights with state reprisals and believed rights to be something they should shun (Chua 2019a).

Similarly, somewhat elusive yet discernible modes of control could lead to insidious effects at this end of the spectrum. Weiss's (2011) study of student activism in Malaysia illustrates this phenomenon fittingly. To curb student activism, Malaysian public universities censored curricula, politicised academic appointments, shortened graduation requirements and precluded 'sensitive' issues – what I describe as agenda-setting measures. Eventually, these agenda-setting measures organised away decades-long history of vibrant campus activism and led to further-reaching implications. They achieved intellectual containment of subsequent generations of students and disciplined the once-feisty university student into a gullible youth who had to beware the undesirable influence of activism. In the case of Singapore, I learned in my study that most activists were reluctant to violate laws that curb speech and assembly, and some even believed that civil disobedience – violating those very restrictions – would discredit their cause (Chua 2014). As a result, they might have quietly submitted themselves to an elusive control whereby they would and should only express dissent in ways permitted or tolerated by the state.

In addition, elusive controls can come in the form of rhetoric about 'cultural' virtue. Southeast Asian scholars, for instance, have exposed the state-sanctioned rhetoric of 'harmony' from Indonesia (Lev 2000), 'social stability' from Singapore (Chua 2014) and 'Asian values' by architects of Southeast Asian authoritarianism (Weiss and Saliha 2003) as cultural window-dressing to discourage rights activism and justify to outsiders why their governments severely curb political freedoms.[15] Others have denounced the authority of Theravada Buddhist kings, monks and other elites, who are supposedly deserving of their high ranks for having accumulated good karma from their past lives (Reynolds 1994). It is, argues Haberkorn (2011), because of such 'cultural' justifications – respect for their high social status and the preservation of 'harmony' – that Thailand's ruling elites who ordered the murders of peasants and students during the uprising of 1973 still enjoy impunity decades after.

---

[15] Also see Nader (2001) on her critique of harmony as a form of social control.

At non-state sites of authoritarianism based on family, marriage, gender, religion and other orders, insidious modes of controls are also quietly at work. In Thailand, legal anthropologists note that 'harmony' and 'respect' blend with Theravada Buddhist precepts of selflessness, non-aggression and forgiveness and instil in people a recipe of moral superiority not to pursue legally entitled rights (Engel and Engel 2010). However, to outsiders looking in, rights simply appear to lack cultural resonance. Likewise, in Kent's (2011) study discussed earlier, the Cambodian women who avoided confronting their attackers in state courts but sought 'moral rehabilitation' in Buddhist temples have perhaps submitted themselves to elusive social controls centred around a patriarchal, misogynistic religious order.

Expanding our horizons to all kinds of authoritarian sites and paying attention to the social practices of controls set an awfully dire scene for rights mobilisation. Given the all-over nature of authoritarianism and the multitude of social controls, how do the weak and marginalised come to recognise their suffering as grievances for which someone or something else is to blame, decide to resist their conditions and, specifically, resist by taking up rights mobilisation? We turn to these concerns in the next section.

3 Power and Resistance

Above and beyond structural conditions, resistance generally and rights mobilisation specifically rest on subjective conditions – how people deal with authoritarianism and its effects on their lives or those whom they care about. Notwithstanding the prevalence of social controls, individuals and groups have mustered courage and wit to challenge authoritarianism. The existence or increase of social controls does not necessarily discourage rights mobilisation. Nor does the relaxation of controls necessarily encourage it. Southeast Asians have mobilised with and for rights innovatively and stubbornly where social controls have persisted and have even tightened.

Thus the questions for this section – *How do people mobilise rights and what forms does rights mobilisation take?* – focus on the second feature of politics of rights, the interplays between structural and subjective conditions, and the third feature, plural practices of rights. We start with orientations and shifts of subjective conditions that motivate the oppressed to take up rights mobilisation. Then we look at the expansive repertoire of rights practices, generated by contestations at plural sites of authoritarianism in Southeast Asia. The diverse practices span formal to non-formal, hidden to openly confrontational and scattered, individual acts to coordinated and collective efforts, stretching rights repertoire far beyond the iconic images of litigation and street protests in Western liberal democracies.

3.1 Agency and Authoritarianism

On one hand, agency is not free-floating but embedded in sites of authoritarian power. On the other, structural conditions of authoritarianism are not entirely determinative. Informed by their social positions and past interactions with other humans and structural conditions, people express and perform agency in heterogenous ways. They might acquiesce, collaborate or collude with authoritarian power, and they might resist (Ortner 2008). It is possible to stop repeating the practices of social controls, mount resistance and, in some cases, mobilise rights. In other words, it is possible to assemble alternative practices using a different recipe of resources from existing structures as well as from newer practices – which may or may not eventually constitute structures – already circulating at a given site.

The decision to resist requires an ideological and behavioural orientation (Levitsky 2014) which recognises the grievance in question, blames a wrongdoer and asserts claims against them. Specifically for rights mobilisation, the decision entails acknowledging the grievance as a rights-related problem, identifying the rights violator or party who should or could offer rights protection and making rights claims directed at them. This kind of ideological and behavioural orientation can take shape as the result of having acquired fresh resources, such as picking up new knowledge or meeting 'transformative agents' (Albiston 2005) – activists, lawyers, friends, family or other people who provide novel information and perspectives.[16] The encounters help those suffering under authoritarianism to re-envision their circumstances, reimagine the potential of available resources and galvanise them to resist (see, e.g., Chua 2019a), changes of heart and mind described by social movements scholars as cognitive liberation (McAdam 1999) and oppositional consciousness (Mansbridge and Morris 2001).

Hence, the exercise of agency to shift ideological and behavioural orientation towards rights mobilisation generates dynamics that deviate from present interplays between the structural and subjective. Having initiated the shift, rights mobilisers continue to adjust their own interpretations of structural conditions and calibrations of audience and opponents. They might attempt a practice, revise it, discard it and try something else – or return to it later. The new interplays thus continue to mutate and evolve as mobilisers respond to the outcomes of their earlier acts of mobilisation and subsequent changes to structural conditions (related or unrelated to their actions).

Some structural conditions of authoritarianism, effectuated by social controls, give rise to the suffering at which rights claims – if and when invoked – are

---

[16] Of course, changes to heart and mind can also occur as a result of self-reflection without new encounters, and they would also count as shifts in the ideological and behavioural orientation of one's agency.

directed: for instance, abuse and killings, discrimination and persecution, poverty and indigence, deprivation and displacement, destruction and seizures of property, devastation and decimation of the environment and denial and erasure of identity. Other structural conditions of authoritarianism suppress rights mobilisation, limiting the capacity and inclination to make rights claims: for instance, censoring information about rights or sanctioning speech, assembly, organisation and other activities associated with resistance and mobilisation. To be sure, structural conditions can both operate as a cause for substantive grievances and constrain rights mobilisation; for example, a gag on political speech can be as much the source of the complaint as it can be a muzzle on speech levelled against the gag itself.

Consequently, Southeast Asians mobilise *for* rights targeted at their grievances, and they also mobilise *with* rights to empower and encourage themselves or others to overcome the suppression of rights mobilisation, so that they can go on to mobilise for rights. In Southeast Asia – and probably in any context – the extensive presence of authoritarianism at state and non-state sites and its selective impact on differently situated people demonstrate that it is, in fact, vital to scrutinise both types of mobilisation. In any case, the influences of authoritarian power on substantive grievances and mobilisation may not be easily separable; in the earlier example on political speech, an act of mobilisation against the gag could target both the complaint about speech and the constraint on mobilisation.

Ultimately, Southeast Asians attempt all sorts of rights practices to address two types of issues that roughly map onto Fraser's (1995) discussion of redistribution and recognition: quotidian and material needs, which are pressing for the rural poor, urban disenfranchised and long-time inhabitants of Southeast Asia's hinterlands; and desires 'to be treated like human' or to get justice and dignity that are frequently deprived of women; ethnic, religious, sexual and gender minorities; the differently abled; and other historically marginalised groups in Southeast Asian societies. The two types of concerns are intertwined, their distinction intended more for analytical than practical purposes. If a person gets more access to resources, employment or shelter, they could make ends meet and thus could feel more dignified, as though they are 'more human.' If no longer deemed an immoral or lesser being, they could more easily obtain opportunities to improve their living standards and find safety and security.[17]

---

[17] Because recognition requires the differentiation of one group from the rest, Fraser (1995) argues, demand for recognition can divert from material redistribution, whereas redistribution promotes de-differentiation by calling for similar distribution of resources across all groups regardless of who they are. Fraser has been criticized for over-polarizing recognition and redistribution, both overlooking the fact that social movements who claim for recognition do care about

By tailoring rights practices to their particular sites of authoritarianism, Southeast Asians produce and accumulate a broad repertoire. Although studies based in Western democracies, especially the United States, do examine rights mobilisation beyond courtroom action, they tend to revolve around judicial decisions; scholars would examine how activists organised a litigation campaign or how they made subsequent use of a court ruling to further their advocacy. Litigation does occur in Southeast Asia, and scholars who study Southeast Asia certainly have covered litigation in their research (see Section 3.1.4). Nonetheless, studies from the region embrace a wider assortment of rights practices overall. Accounting for tight social controls that modulate from being explicitly brutal to elusive, rights practices in Southeast Asia do not always aim at formal legal reform. They include acts of self-preservation, efforts to change hearts and minds and grassroots organisation to recruit followers and shore up support.

3.2 The Repertoire of Rights Practices

We can organise the expansive repertoire of rights practices in Southeast Asia – and arguably other places – based on three characteristics: degree of coordination, degree of openness and degree of formality.

- Degree of coordination refers to whether the practice was carried out individually (and thus uncoordinated) or implemented collectively (and thus orchestrated). The participants of coordinated resistance need not possess exactly the same concrete goals, but they should share a common understanding of their structural conditions and mutual desire to improve them.
- Degree of openness refers to whether mobilisers conceal from or reveal to those in positions of authoritarian power the intention to challenge their power. Covert or hidden actions could lay the foundation for bolder, collective action, though they could also re-emerge following open, contentious resistance.
- Degree of formality refers to whether mobilisers employ formal or official channels of the state, such as litigating in the courts, lobbying the legislature or filing complaints with administrative agencies; quasi-formal methods, such as consulting lawyers, which could lead to the pursuit of formal means; or nonformal means such as street protests and recruitment and training at the grassroots.

This broad repertoire would largely fit the topography of tactics in the study of contentious politics (Tilly and Tarrow 2007), except that it encompasses not

---

redistribution and neglecting the connection between material recourse and cultural changes (Young 1997).

only the collective – the emphasis in contentious politics – but also the uncoordinated acts of individuals.[18] Its inclusion of covert acts also contravenes conventional wisdom in socio-legal studies of politics of rights, which typically focus on open forms of mobilisation. On the other hand, this repertoire would be consistent with typologies of resistance that embrace both rowdy crowd protests and subversive, individual acts (see, e.g., Hollander and Einwohner 2004).

We can imagine the degrees of coordination, openness and formality as three intersecting axes (Figure 2). In the three-dimensional space demarcated by the axes, we would plot rights practices according to where they land along each axis – individual to collective, overt to covert and formal to non-formal means. An attribute on one axis does not presuppose the attributes on the other two axes, though some attributes – for example, hidden, uncoordinated and non-formal – are more likely to go together.

Where to place a practice in this three-dimensional space is a subjective exercise and fluctuates depending on the actor or beholder. What is peaceful protest to mobilisers could be too confrontational and therefore intolerably transgressive to a paranoid state, as epitomised by the Myanmar military dictatorship (Cheesman 2021). My judgement call on how to mark a certain practice is based on my standpoint as a scholar combining the emic and etic

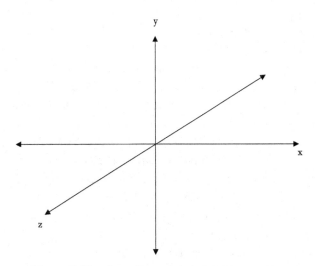

Figure 2 *The three dimensions of rights practices*

---

[18] In addition, Tilly and Tarrow (2007) require the involvement of interactions with agents of government in contentious politics, which is usually not a necessary criterion in rights mobilisation research.

sensibilities considered earlier. For ease of discussion, I have organised the rights practices gathered from my own research and other Southeast Asian research into four subsections.

3.2.1 Uncoordinated, Hidden and (Mostly) Informal

When social controls are overwhelmingly severe, the weak may have little freedom or ability to articulate their grievances, much less put up any form of resistance. They may decide that the costs of challenging explicit bans or implicit rules are too huge for their livelihood and physical safety – or the well-being of their loved ones. For those who nevertheless want to alleviate their situation or prevent its further deterioration but hesitate to alter existing power relations due to the perceived risk and cost, they might opt for uncoordinated and hidden practices. Most of the time, these practices are non-formal and deliberately concealed from or located far away from formal channels.

Famously characterised as 'everyday resistance' in Scott's (1984) ethnography of a Malay village on peninsular Malaysia, uncoordinated, hidden tactics include foot dragging, dissimulation, desertion, false compliance, pilfering, feigned ignorance, slander and sabotage. The peasants in Scott's book faced sanctions and threats such as rent hikes, increased taxes and outright violence. They were also expected to follow the normative order governing the inherently unequal relationship between landlord and tenant. Instead of openly and directly fighting these social controls, the peasants resisted their landlords' conduct with 'weapons of the weak', which stopped short of outright confrontation with authority, required little or no coordination and took advantage of implicit, shared understandings of power relations (Scott 1984, p. xvi).[19]

Unsurprisingly, given the odds of authoritarianism stacked against them, uncoordinated, hidden tactics are common among peasants (see, e.g., Caouette and Turner 2009), labourers (see, e.g., Bal 2015) and ethnic minorities (see, e.g., Ho and Chua 2016; Turner and Michaud 2009) in Southeast Asia. Bal (2015) describes how migrant construction workers in Singapore 'deliver a facade of obedient and competent work whilst engaging in covert "everyday resistances" for two reasons – to siphon better rewards (wages, tenure, deployments) from work superiors and to avoid open conflict with them' (p. 275). The workers selectively work faster during cooler parts of the day to exceed expectations and prove their competence to supervisors and then slack off during mid-day when there is no supervision. In Kerkvliet's (2005) study of northern Vietnam, villagers pushed back against a collective farming policy by

---

[19] For a different treatment of 'resistance' that is also built on Southeast Asian–based studies, see Prasse-Freeman (2020).

doing less or not doing what they were supposed to do, quietly forcing the communist government to abandon the policy. In Brunei, Malays who refused to conform to Muslim practices dodged surveillance to continue with traditional shrine worship, exorcism and other outlawed practices. They would visit the outlawed shrines secretly at night or early in the morning, or they would drive by and toss their offerings from the car windows (Muller 2015).

Granted, not all hidden practices featured in Southeast Asian literature involve rights claims. However, the scope of rights mobilisation can accommodate hidden practices that meet its definition. Whether a covert resister was indeed mobilising rights is an empirical question. Similar to how we would discern everyday resistance more generally, we would search for the answer to the resister's intention in our fieldwork data, including interviews and observations of behaviour. Was the resister interpreting and expressing their discontent in rights' terms? When a peasant reported reaping less harvest in order to pay less taxes, did the peasant believe they had a right or thought their right had been violated by their landlord? If so, they would be carrying out rights mobilisation. Hidden practices of rights should not be discounted because they are too troublesome to verify or too odd for the standard rights toolbox. 'If we allow ourselves to call only [open, radical political activity] "resistance", we simply allow the structure of domination to define for us what is resistance and what is not resistance' (Scott 1984, p. 299).[20]

3.2.2 Coordinated, Hidden and (Mostly) Non-formal

Like individual everyday resisters, mobilisers who practise rights in coordinated, hidden fashion want to conceal their intention of challenging authoritarianism. Their rights practices resemble those of covert resistance and tend to be non-formal in nature, especially when aimed at official actors. At the same time, unlike individual everyday resisters, these mobilisers have managed to overcome to some extent the social controls on group-based activities, such as assembly and association, and do not operate in isolation but collaborate with one another.

In my study on Singapore's gay rights movement, I found that activists perform a type of coordinated, hidden practice I call 'pragmatic resistance' (Chua 2014). They collectively and covertly disguise their resistant intention, avoid coming across to state actors as confrontational or threatening and settle for small, creeping gains. The annual public gathering Pink Dot vividly illustrates the features of pragmatic resistance. On Pink Dot day, event organisers and other Singaporeans dress up in pink attire, congregate for a picnic and form

---

[20] For contrasting views on whether and how we can gauge the intention behind covert, individual acts of resistance, see Hollander and Einwohner (2004).

a pink human dot. Held since 2009, Pink Dot has become Singapore's alternative to a pride parade, the type of demonstration of which the government disapproves. Staged in a public park, Pink Dot is right out in the open and undoubtedly a massive exercise of coordination. And yet, Pink Dot organisers' resistant intent is somewhat hidden. The park is the only venue in Singapore where public assembly is allowed without prior licensing approval (a social control in the form of channelling).[21] By limiting Pink Dot to the park, the organisers ostensibly have complied with the state's boundaries on public demonstrations; inwardly, however, they know they have resisted the restriction on their right to assembly by creatively pushing its boundaries to the limits.

Many more Southeast Asian attempts at rights mobilisation take on a combination of coordinated/hidden/non-formal attributes. For example, Vietnamese activists who objected to inadequate land compensation would tell funny stories that were both critical of and seemingly non-confrontational towards the one-party state (Gillespie 2018). They painted an idealised village life to pander to the communist party's valorisation of peasants, and they buried within their humour satirical moments about the injustice of the land tenure system – actions that perhaps resemble the performances of 'hidden transcript' (Scott 1990) in which resisters tacitly or explicitly coordinate among themselves to critique their oppressors. In Malseed's (2008) ethnographic study of Karen villages, when Burmese soldiers came demanding laborers or materials, village heads would feign absence or illness or would delay or reduce supply, and farmers would plant and harvest at night to evade detection. Although not every villager treated each action as a step towards a larger, well-articulated goal, Malseed argues, they shared common understandings that they had a right to control their own land, livelihood and identity.

Grassroots organising is another practice that can take place in coordinated, hidden fashion (it can also take place openly, and, when it does, it would go into the coordinated, overt cluster that will be examined last). Grassroots organising is coordinated because at least two persons are expected to act in concert: the person adapting and communicating ideas about rights; and the person engaging with the communicator and information. And it is carried out covertly when mobilisers want to circumvent censorship or avoid punishment from the state or other authoritarians. Thus, in the 2000s, Burmese rights activists got around social controls on activism by operating out of Thailand and then surreptitiously inviting new recruits across the border to participate in their activities (Chua 2019a). Moreover, by its nature, grassroots organising work typically involves

---

[21] Speakers are required to register in advance with the police and to abide by pre-set conditions, such as steering clear of issues of race or religion that the state deem to be sensitive (Chua 2014).

non-formal methods. To tackle implicit controls that shape beliefs about the unsuitability or inappropriateness of rights, activists would engage in translation (Merry 2006) or vernacular mobilisation (Chua 2015) to adapt rights into the local context so that they become meaningful to their audience. For instance, Thai activists harmonise international human rights with lived Buddhist concepts of structure and hierarchy, as well as everyday conventions around maintaining 'face', patronage relations and status (Selby 2018); and, Muslim activists in Malaysia render international women's rights discourse more palatable by synthesising it with Islamic jurisprudence and values (Moustafa 2018).

3.2.3 Uncoordinated, Open and Formal-to-Non-formal

Uncoordinated and open forms of rights mobilisation take after the 'rightful resistance' of China's peasants. A term coined by O'Brien and Li (2006), 'rightful resistance' refers to uncoordinated mobilisation that is confrontational, frank about its contentious intent but short of rebellion. Rightful resisters draw upon 'laws, policies, and other officially promoted values to defy disloyal political and economic elites' and make use of 'influential allies and recognised principles to apply pressure on those in power who have failed to live up to a professed ideal or who have not implemented some beneficial measure' (O'Brien and Li 2006, pp. 2–3). The latitude of formality-to-non-formality is much wider among uncoordinated and open practices of rights, and we are likely to notice a mix of formal, non-formal and quasi-formal methods.

In studies on Southeast Asian societies, we can find rightful resisters who directly challenge written laws and unwritten political norms. Yet, because they are appealing to what they believe could be derived from or granted by official policies, laws, principles and legitimating ideologies, they are playing simultaneously to and within existing normative orders. Therefore, in Nguyen's (2018) study of Vietnamese labour rights, when factory workers composed letters to the labour inspector to complain about their employers' illegal conduct and to hold the government accountable for their plight, they referred to labour rights legislation as well as the communist party's representation of itself as the vanguard of equality and progress. In terms of degree of formality, their act of letter-writing could be regarded as quasi-formal in that it did not go through a formal forum but nevertheless formally addressed an official actor.

Apart from urban labourers, rural residents and peasants have attempted rightful resistance in Southeast Asia. For instance, the Khmu in Laos urged the national government to halt its land reclamation plans by citing to legal provisions and requesting a sympathetic governor to write to the National Assembly to argue that the land concessions had not been properly effected (McAllister 2015).

Whereas the Khmu's tactics resemble those of the workers in Nguyen's study, the actions of Burmese villagers in Prasse-Freeman (2016), demonstrating with placards against state reclamation of their land, typify the non-formal means of protest. More intriguingly, Prasse-Freeman observes that these villagers did not merely rely on rights already recognised in state law, the hallmark of rightful resistance. By putting up 'rule of law' signboards that imitate official warnings against trespass on state land, Prasse-Freeman surmises, they were demanding Burmese authorities to enforce black-letter law to uphold their land rights. In doing so, they were also expressing their aspiration for rule of law, which is seldom upheld in Myanmar. Hence, in Prasse-Freeman's study, we can detect a slightly expanded scope of rightful resistance. The villagers did not link their arguments to state law, ruling party rhetoric or other official norms but to their own understandings (Kerkvliet 2014) of land ownership and rule of law, which could be informed by non-normative orders unsanctioned by the state.

Furthermore, in Prasse-Freeman's study, the erection of similar signs hints at cooperation among the resisters, adding one more variation to rightful resistance. Another example along similar lines is Taylor's (2014) research on Khmer minorities at the Cambodian-Vietnamese border. To demand the return of their land, Khmer residents travelled together to Ho Chi Minh City, where they protested and met with central government officials to accuse local bureaucrats of failing to live up to their duties and the communist party's ideals. Although the author did not explicitly frame the Khmers' actions as rightful resistance, it is plausible to describe them as such. Due to the presence of cooperation among the villagers in Prasse-Freeman and Taylor's studies, we would place their rights practices closer to the coordinated end of the uncoordinated-coordinated axis but not to the extent of sustained orchestrations found in social movements.

3.2.4 Coordinated, Open and Formal-to-Non-formal

Mobilisers who practice rights openly and collectively do not cover up their intention to resist authoritarianism. The longer they sustain their coordination, the more likely their acts of collective mobilisation would amount to those of a social movement, and the more likely they would refine and articulate their intentions.[22] In Southeast Asia, despite explicit social controls on confrontational acts of resistance, open and collective forms of rights mobilisation are far from uncommon. These practices usually include the non-formal means of street protest and the classic representation of formal means, litigation.[23]

---

[22] Coordinated and open tactics can also escalate into revolutions and armed insurgencies.

[23] Litigation can also be the acts of lone individuals, which would fall within the cluster of uncoordinated, open and formal.

Additionally, grassroots organisation might take place overtly when activists deem their structural conditions to be safe enough to do so. Thus, Burmese activists were able to hold human rights workshops and public events under the rule of the semi-civilian government for about a decade, before the country once again fell to military dictatorship in 2021.

Burmese youths who confronted the military in the wake of the 2021 coup and in 1988 against the then military-led totalitarian regime would most probably belong high on the list of street protests carried out in the face of dangerous authoritarian conditions in Southeast Asia. A less extreme example would be the Malaysian Hindu Rights Action Force (HINDRAF) campaign for racial justice and equality. Regardless of the state's curtailments on public assembly, HINDRAF leaders mustered thousands of Malaysian Indians to flock to the capital city and presented a petition to the British High Commissioner, requesting for a Queen's Counsel to act for descendants of Indian indentured labourers in British Malaya in a lawsuit against the British government (Kananatu 2020). A still more cautious case would be that of Singaporean gay rights activists, who first cultivated experience and confidence with covert practices before mobilising more openly. In Section 3.1.2 on coordinated, hidden and non-formal tactics, I explained that the organisers of Pink Dot, by obeying the social controls on freedom of assembly and speech, kept the resistant intent of the annual gathering partially covert. Nonetheless, after a decade of interplay between structural and subjective conditions, Pink Dot appears to have gradually become more outspoken. At their most recent instalments, Pink Dot organisers announced their support for constitutional rights litigation and called on the government – albeit politely and friendlily – to decriminalise consensual same-sex relations. They have remained law-abiding, have continued to adhere to the restriction on their rights to speech and assembly and have not expressed any intent to violate the law, but they have also progressively disclosed their rights aspirations for sexual minorities (Chua 2014).

As for litigation, although scholars have shown that Southeast Asians avoid the courts due to their lack of time and familiarity with the formal legal order (see, e.g., Grenfell 2015) or its corrupt and abusive practices (see, e.g., Cheesman 2015), some have filed lawsuits and battled it out with their opponents in court. Scholars have written about litigation campaigns for a variety of issues in both domestic and foreign courts. There are lawsuits that go against the state, such as the Indonesian government to hold it accountable for inequality in education (Rosser 2015); the Malaysian state and federal governments for purportedly violating the right to freedom of religion, particularly apostasy and conversion out of Islam in Malaysia (Moustafa 2018); the Singaporean government for allegedly failing to uphold the constitutional rights to equality and personal liberty by maintaining the criminalisation of same-sex relations (Chua 2017); and Filipino agencies in defence of Indigenous peoples' rights against hard-rock mining (Holden 2005). There are also lawsuits that target corporations, such as pharmaceutical companies for the right to access to treatment in Thailand (Ford et al. 2009) and the oil corporation UNOCAL in American courts for the abuse of human rights of Burmese farmers (Dale 2011; Holzmeyer 2009).

Like claimants elsewhere, when they do go to court Southeast Asian litigants often hope for more than a favourable judgment to safeguard formal rights. In addition to achieving the instrumental outcomes of preventing or compelling behaviour, they may try to harness the cultural effects of rights mobilisation, such as to inspire, encourage or rally. Thus, Munger (2014) observes, in the wake of the 1997 constitutional reform in Thailand a group of activist lawyers would select cases to litigate in the newly established constitutional courts so that they could empower activists and influence judges with the spirit and promise of constitutional rights. Meanwhile, for activists who filed a class action against Ferdinand Marcos (who was living in exile in the United States), they not only wanted monetary compensation on behalf of Filipinos whom their former president had tortured and killed but also sought worldwide media attention to expose his wrongdoings (Ela 2017).

Confronted with social controls in varying shapes and force, Southeast Asians who do resist authoritarian power *and* turn to rights mobilisation produce and proliferate a colourful array of rights practices that spans a wide range in coordination, openness and formality. Have these practices borne fruit? Can they? Having surveyed the vast inventory of rights practices that people in this region have accumulated in pursuit of their needs and desires for a better life, we move on to the final section to consider the effects of rights mobilisation and how we should assess its consequences.

4 Power of Rights

We can identify and assess the effects of rights mobilisation based on the instrumental and cultural powers of rights. Instrumental effects, which are more easily quantifiable, originate from rights' power to reward and punish. They include enactments of state legislation or amendments to existing provisions, court judgments that recognise claimants' rights and the penalising and curbing of right-violating behaviour. Cultural effects, usually assessable through the use of qualitative, interpretive fieldwork, emanate from rights' symbolic (McCann 1994) or connotative power (Goodale 2007). Socio-legal scholars trace the motivations, emotions, words and actions of rights claimants, as well as those of their opponents and other relevant audiences, to discern changes to identity, discourses and meanings. Cultural changes are inherently valuable, but they can also lay the groundwork to achieve instrumental effects in the longer run. Therefore, from the perspective of politics of rights, even when rights' direct, instrumental impact is impaired, rights mobilisation can contribute to social change by virtue of their symbolic or connotative power to inspire, encourage and rally people to '(re)formulate, (re)think about, and react to political problems' (Scheingold 2004, p. 14; parentheses added).

Because rights practices materialise from interplays of structural and subjective conditions involving differently situated people, any consequence – irrespective of whether it is instrumental or cultural – would vary from place to place, time to time and practice to practice, as well as among individuals and groups. The literature from Southeast Asia confirms this general takeaway in socio-legal studies: rights can vindicate the oppressed, empower the weak and redress grievances, but they can also backfire or turn out to be ineffective, ultimately disempowering or disillusioning those who look to their protection. In other words, we find a mix of gains and critiques, sometimes described by socio-legal scholars as the paradoxical quality of rights (McCann 2014). Critical scholars who take the view that rights are Global North constructions would add that, more than being ineffectual, the pervasiveness of rights can be so harmful as to occlude other ways of thinking about and solving problems, often at the expense of native solutions and ideas. Therefore, critical scholars contend, rights reinforce the unequal power relations between the Global North and South and between local elites and the rest of the population.

We examine these gains and critiques of rights mobilisation and conclude with my position on its mixed outcomes and critical scholars' problem with the hegemony of rights. For me, the way out of the thorny debate for and against rights lies with the empirically informed approach of politics of rights, being attentive to the presence of plural sites of authoritarianism, the interplay between structural and subjective conditions and the existence of plural practices of rights. With this premise, I offer a plea for rights, one that accepts their flaws and their potential. The central questions of this section – *What are the consequences of rights mobilisation and how do we assess them?* – thus bring us full circle. We pull together all three features of politics of rights and draw upon our emic and etic sensibilities to help us make sense of the possibilities and promise of rights and to appreciate with compassion the agency of the weak and marginalised in the face of authoritarianism.

4.1 Gains from Rights Mobilisation

In spite of widespread authoritarianism, rights mobilisation in Southeast Asia has frequently turned out to be rewarding. Running the gamut of formal to non-formal, the rights practices of Southeast Asians have achieved instrumental and cultural changes. Some changes directly go to structural conditions or authoritarian practices of social controls. Others affect subjective conditions, which may go on to influence social practices followed by structural conditions.

Instrumental gains include compelling behaviour that provides for improved security or quality of life. Formal tactics such as lobbies have pushed legislators to reform labour law (Caraway and Ford 2020); and litigation has enabled parents to hold the government accountable for inequality in education (Rosser 2015) and allowed abused women to divorce and find refuge from their estranged husbands (Curnow 2015). Non-formal tactics such as protests have halted dam building (Shirley and Word 2018) and mass tree-felling (Gillespie and Nguyen 2019), whereas quiet, uncoordinated resistance of peasants has cumulatively broken down national agrarian policies (Kerkvliet 2005). In these aforementioned cases, some of the instrumental effects reshape structural conditions of authoritarianism directly – for example, by altering the legal order with enhanced rights protection for livelihood and safer living environments – whereas other instrumental effects inhibit immediate practices of social controls, such as domestic violence against women.

Incremental, less-visible cultural transformations often begin with one's sense of self and social relationships. Rights mobilisers have demonstrated that grassroots efforts at recruitment and education, for example, can increase self-worth and self-efficacy. Thus, newcomers to the Burmese LGBT rights movement (Chua 2019a), after having spent time learning about rights advocacy from the movement's leaders, started to think of themselves as equal to heterosexual, cisgender Burmese and then grew in self-esteem as they took up leadership roles in the movement. In his ethnography of Indigenous environmental movements in southwestern Philippines, Theriault (2011) described a young man who redefined his identity as a Pala'wan after joining an Indigenous rights group and gaining exposure to Indigenous rights legislation. The young man ran for office and became the first Indigenous councillor from his village. These cultural transformations at the personal level are modifications to subjective conditions that could gradually destabilise entrenched normative orders. Picture women in a patriarchal society believing they are men's equals and conducting themselves according to that belief (Olivius and Hedström 2019) or small-time tenant farmers seeing through the once-taken-for-granted, hierarchical landlord–peasant relationship for its abuse and exploitation (Diprose and McGregor 2009). When the subordinate start to doubt the authority or legitimacy behind social controls over morality, economic production or social hierarchy, they become less and less likely to comply or accept them, loosening the capacity of social controls to safeguard entrenched normative orders.

Starting from the personal level, cultural transformations can induce broader ramifications. They can spread to more people, paving the way for more activism and bolder tactics as similarly transformed individuals come together to pool ideas, skills and money to mobilise collectively. For instance, villagers scattered across isolated communities on Negros Island, the Philippines, banded together upon the encouragement and tutelage of rights activists and eventually combined financial resources to sue their landowners for rights violations (Diprose and McGregor 2009); and, transgender women in Malaysia known as *mak nyah* collaborated with lawyers to challenge the constitutionality of a shariah law in the federated state of Negeri Sembilan that prohibited 'cross-dressing' (Goh and Kananatu 2019). These contestations against structural conditions could also influence subjective conditions more broadly, such that the public would begin to reconsider their actions and thoughts that contribute to social controls. For example, although the villagers could not entirely decommission the Pak Mun Dam site in northeastern Thailand, their vehement protests attracted nationwide attention and forced urban Thais to reflect on the calamity that big state-sponsored projects bring to outlying communities (Kuhonta 2009).

Furthermore, cultural transformations at the collective level, particularly by reinterpreting injuries and grievances as rights violations, can attract the assistance of transnational organisations and strengthen rights mobilisers' ability to attain greater changes. According to Goh and Kananatu (2019), even though Malaysian courts dismissed the constitutional rights claims of the *mak nyah*, their rights practices solidified their status as a collective distinct from other gender and sexual minorities and drew international NGOs to their cause. Another illustration is the Cordillerans from the mountainous region of Northern Luzon, the Philippines. As one of the first groups in Asia to cast themselves as Indigenous and join the global Indigenous rights movements, the Cordillerans earned a platform at the United Nations and built international alliances to help pressure the Filipino government into drafting Indigenous rights legislation (Bertrand 2011).

4.2 Critiques of Rights Mobilisation

Nonetheless, scholars have also raised questions about the effectiveness of rights mobilisation. They have uncovered evidence of failures to achieve or retain instrumental wins as well as exposed the pitfalls of trying to harness cultural transformation. Aspinall's (2019) description of progressive movements in post-Suharto Indonesia is aptly applicable to rights mobilisation throughout the region: 'It often recalls the labours of Sisyphus, with most of the gains . . . fragile and insecure, under recurrent threat of rollback and constant pressure of erosion. Progress in one sector or region is frequently matched by regression in another' (p. 188). Rights mobilisation has frequently failed to achieved its intended effects and, in some instances, led to unintended consequences to the mobilisers' detriment.

Side by side with treaty ratifications, formal legal reform and the establishment of national human rights institutions are reports of international NGOs[24] and scholarly literature, their pages filled with the instrumental setbacks of rights mobilisation. The best-intentioned measures meant to improve structural conditions flounder when state actors, family patriarchs, big businesses or other authoritarian parties persist with their social controls. To name a few examples: in Indonesia, the laws enacted by provincial and national governments to protect the rights of people with disabilities lack teeth, Dibley (2019) points out, as policymakers drag their feet on enforcement and execution. Meanwhile, Irianto (2004) observes, Batak families frequently ignore the equal property rights of women in Indonesian state law and continue to divide property based on their non-state, patriarchal normative order. In Myanmar, Mark (2016) documents how the military disenfranchised small farmers who held formal land rights by awarding to corporations large concessions for the same plots of land. Other well-intended structural changes are not realised because they neglect the more deeply embedded effects of authoritarianism. For instance, the Indigenous Agta in the Philippines enjoy the formal right to participate in decisions affecting resources on state-protected lands where they dwell but in reality exercise little influence. The Agta do not receive notice of the meetings in time, have no money to travel to and from the meetings and cannot communicate effectively in English when they do manage to attend (Minter et al. 2014) – issues connected to long-term social controls that have marginalised them economically and socially.

Moreover, when conservative factions perceive that their moral superiority, economic advantage or social standing is under threat, they have reacted violently against rights mobilisers. For example, regressive crusades in Indonesia have intensified in correlation with the proliferation of such progressive movements as disability rights, women's rights, student activism, labour

---

[24] International bodies such as Amnesty International, Human Rights Watch and the United Nations publish reports regularly on Southeast Asian states and the region.

rights, urban poor, land and anti-corruption (Fealy 2019). In Malaysia, whenever liberal rights groups challenged the jurisdiction of shariah courts over the marital and custodial affairs of non-Muslims (who were formerly Muslims or married to Muslims), conservative Islamic groups have attacked and accused them of conspiring to weaken their religion (Moustafa 2018). The opponents in such cases either pressure an already authoritarian state to stifle rights mobilisers' claims or directly apply social controls, like physical violence and formal laws that have sustained authoritarianism in their favour.

Other scholars express concerns over the harnessing of rights' symbolic power to produce cultural effects, worrying that these rights practices end up reinforcing normative orders and social controls that constitute existing authoritarian structures. When mobilisers adapt rights to a given authoritarian site, in order to gain traction, earn approval or better persuade state actors, opponents and other audiences, they would typically draw from resources from the same normative orders against which they are resisting. Although the creative reassembling of resources into rights practices could reap the rewards described earlier, it inevitably engages on the authoritarian's turf (McCann 2020). According to this argument, mobilisers play by or accept, to varying degrees, some of the terms of the authoritarian structures, consequently reinforcing some of its social controls on moral, economic and social orders. To illustrate, Singaporean LGBT rights activists who enacted 'pragmatic resistance' conform to the state's written and unwritten rules on how to behave as a dissenter (Chua 2014); similarly, migrant rights activists who rely on pragmatic resistance-esque tactics leave intact Singapore's conservative race-based immigration regime (Kemp and Kfir 2016) and do not dispute its underlying problems of class, gender, ethnicity and citizenship (Lyons 2005). At non-state sites of authoritarianism, we can come across similar concerns. For instance, Cambodian women who lead the charge on land rights activism receive respect and praise, but they do so by presenting themselves as patriarchal definitions of women as wives, mothers and stewards of family unity and safety (Park 2018). As one commentator said about young Malay women who complained about 'female' problems to escape the discipline and surveillance of the factory floor (Ong 2010), such acts of resistance are concomitantly reinscriptions of traditional gendered stereotypes (Freeman 2010) set by prevailing gender orders that control women's 'morality' or social position.[25]

---

[25] The first edition of Ong's (2010) well-known ethnography was published in 1987 and did not refer to everyday resistance to describe the conduct of young female factory workers who complained of 'female' problems, requested prayer time and reported falling prey to angry spirits. However, their actions can be regarded as 'hidden tactics of resistance' (Freeman 2010)

The (re)invention of rights-associated identities has also attracted parallel criticisms about buttressing authoritarian structures. As part of their rights practices, mobilisers in Southeast Asia may modify identities or create new labels, such as a particular Indigenous or ethnic minority, people with disabilities or LGBT individuals, to unite a population and render them recognisable as a rights-bearing group. Critics argue that this kind of identity (re)inventions could flatten the complexities within a people and play into social controls that stereotype and 'other' marginalised populations. In Southeast Asia, Indigenous rights mobilisation illustrates this conundrum well. For groups who claim Indigenous rights from national governments and alliances from international bodies, despite having altered customary practices and lifestyles as they moved around and exploited resources (Zerner 1994), 'Indigenous' groups realised that they had to keep on proving their indigeneity (Brosius 2003) – as savages, slash-and-burn agriculturists and spiritual kindreds of land dating back to time immemorial – and that the more apparently exotic Indigenous populations look to lowlanders, such as by adorning 'traditional' dress and headgear that they would not wear in everyday life, the more likely they would be heard by government officials (Paredes 2019). As a result, Indigenous rights advocacy could risk locking the Indigenous into 'traditional' livelihoods (Dressler 2009; Li 2000).

4.3 The Problem of Rights Hegemony

Critical scholars argue that the contradictory outcomes of rights mobilisation, its effectiveness and drawbacks, form a paradox to sustain rights as an all-encompassing influence, a hegemonic normative order that does more harm than good for the marginalised who pursue them. The specific criticisms and emphases vary, but they can be summarised as follows: the occasional victories ameliorate the more frequent pangs of defeat and offer moments of release to keep mobilisers committed to rights' alluring promises and make them believe that rights actually work and offer legitimate, helpful solutions. Mobilisers just need to persevere and improve their practices of rights. Nonetheless, their pursuit of rights ultimately props up the very authoritarian structures and those in power who have contributed to their grievances. In short, applying the language of this Element to the critical rights perspective, rights practices amount to the construction of authoritarian structures – those of rights.[26]

---

to extract temporary relief from the assembly line and to diminish the control of male supervisors.

[26] Golder (2015), however, observes that some critical scholars on the radical left have recently shifted their positions to depict rights as a tactical opening that could lead to other forms of emancipation, restatements and struggles.

What is so detrimental about subscribing wholeheartedly to rights and pursuing them? Harms' (2016) ethnography of two master-planned urban development projects located on either side of the Phú Mỹ Bridge in Ho Chi Minh City, Vietnam, provides an evocative account. Phú Mỹ Hưng is a completed, luxurious urban living space, while Thủ Thiêm is an incomplete construction site whose residents had been evicted or displaced by the development. The residents at both sites insisted on their property rights with starkly different outcomes. Boosted by the success of their claims, Phú Mỹ Hưng residents demonstrated an emergent sense of individualistic rights and went on to wield their land rights to exclude others from staking claims on their property. Thủ Thiêm residents were unsuccessful with their land rights claims, and yet they persisted with their fight for compensation. Inhabitants at both sites, therefore, had bought into the promise of rights and fuelled a belief that people who lost their homes to big commercial developments could receive monetary compensation, even though Thủ Thiêm's case exemplifies just how frequently such claims have failed. Ultimately, Harms argues, the surging rights discourse enabled a rapacious land market that threatens to dispossess and displace more ordinary Vietnamese.

For Southeast Asia and other parts of the Global South, the critical rights perspective can be further explicated through TWAIL (Third World Approaches to International Law), whose arguments generally run as follows: Global North international organisations and funders often require 'good governance' to ensure the proper implementation of their economic or technical assistance. As human rights projects in disguise, good governance mandates changes to the recipient country's legal or political orders, such as the enactment of rights legislation and procedures in compliance with international rights standards; consequently, the globalisation of rights from North to South could exacerbate the unequal distribution of power (Anghie 2004). Materially, Global South nations are compelled to implement rights agenda conditionally tied to developmental aid; culturally, top-down rights programmes displace alternative solutions that could be more radical, less individualistic or – at least – homegrown. When tied to neo-capitalist projects, such top-down rights programmes tend to settle for preventing or mitigating deprivations and accept the structural conditions of neo-capitalism that had caused and reproduced those sufferings (Linarelli, Salomon and Sornarajah 2018).

Furthermore, in line with the critical view, top-down rights projects funded by the Global North could exacerbate unequal social orders between the poor and rich or the elite and ordinary masses in Southeast Asia and other Global South regions. For instance, socio-legal studies find that urban elites working in professional NGOs are often the ones who receive money from international or

foreign entities to fund human rights activities and therefore control the movement agenda over their grassroots counterparts (Chua 2019a). For critical
scholars, the inequalities are aggravated if these top-down projects introduce
rights-affiliated identities, such as the aforementioned Indigenous or LGBT
rights identities, to go along with their implementation. In doing so, critical
scholars contend, local activists end up promoting identities that originate from
the Global North, homogenising what used to be diverse, unique local understandings of certain subjectivities, such as gender or sexuality, and sidelining
them for being premodern and unliberated (Massad 2002; Puar 2002).

4.4 From Pluralities to Power of Change

Having weighed the gains and critiques of rights mobilisation, including the
critical perspective on the problem of hegemony, I come out circumspectly on
the side of rights. Despite the ineffectualness of Sisyphus-like labour and the
jeopardies of reinforcing authoritarian structures, rights are hardly a sham.
I arrive at this conclusion by returning to the empirically grounded approach
of politics of rights and its three key features – the presence of state and non-
state sites of authoritarianism with multiple normative orders, some overlapping
and others inconsistent with one another; the ever-contingent interplays
between structural and subjective conditions; and, consequently, plural practices that form a broad and diverse repertoire of rights.

The fate of rights rises and falls in Southeast Asia because of the region's
diversity, its plural political, legal and social orders. In some instances, rights
practices might be powerful enough to eventually overcome social controls and
transform authoritarian conditions. In other cases, the widespread presence of
authoritarianism prevents rights from exerting any overwhelming influence. As
we saw from the examples earlier, governments have simply refused or failed to
adopt rights practices and instead stifled them with retaliation, inaction or
ineptitude, as have authoritarian actors at non-state sites. Moreover, Southeast
Asians do not necessarily devote themselves to rights simply because they are
available. Rather, they have frequently regarded rights as one of many practices
to which they could turn to deal with their problems. A person who has the right
in state law to sue her injurer for compensation could, instead, seek redress
according to her village norms or solace in her religious order and refrain from
taking any action against her injurer (Engel and Engel 2010).[27]

The mixed outcomes of rights mobilisation suggest that, even though it has
triumphed in Southeast Asia from time to time, it has not managed to construct
rights into a hegemonic structure. So far, Southeast Asians' innumerable

---

[27] Also see 'Elusive Modes' of social controls in Section 2, 'Power and Control'.

practices of rights have complicated and further pluralised sites of authoritarianism, adding new dimensions to ways of responding to injuries and injustice (Munger 2006). The same can be said of Southeast Asian creations of rights-affiliated identities, such as LGBT (Chua and Gilbert 2015; Thoreson 2012) or an ethnic minority label like 'Malaysian Hindu' (Kananatu 2020). These identities belong to what has been described as a repository of identities that Southeast Asians switch, use and present as situationally cued (Scott 2009) and in commensuration with the politics of rights at play.

More importantly, in arriving at my conclusion, I am guided by the goal of politics of rights to produce empirically informed, complex and fine-grained analyses of human agency, especially in the face of authoritarianism. Marginalised individuals and groups assess the risks and tailor their responses according to the nature of authoritarianism and the modes of social controls. They might practice rights openly, choose covert strategies or avoid rights altogether. Reticence and reluctance to challenge authoritarianism do not necessarily denote resignation or acquiescence, as the weak may remain keenly aware of their vulnerability to violence and may have exercised agency in this manner precisely to protect themselves (Scott 1984). When they do take up rights mobilisation, they may not necessarily have been duped by rights – that is, fall into critical scholars' alleged trap of hegemony. Rather than attribute decisions regarding mobilisation to unwavering faith in rights, we should explicate why and how mobilisers turn to rights. Conversely, when rights mobilisation does not occur or fails to achieve intended outcomes, we should parse through the workings of social controls to analyse the impact of authoritarianism on the emergence of resistance generally and rights mobilisation specifically.

The project of critiquing the hegemony of rights tends to brush over, on the one hand, the structural conditions and social controls that produce authoritarianism and, on the other hand, the pressing needs of rights mobilisers working under authoritarianism (Liu 2015). From rights mobilisation literature and Southeast Asian studies, we have learned that state and non-state sites of power may help to perpetuate authoritarianism and oppress some or almost all populations within. To these populations, rights can be a viable alternative to counter entrenched norms held up as culture to hold them down and keep them in line with the dominant moral requirements, economic imperatives or political hierarchy. To borrow from Thompson's (1975) conclusion about legal power and the Black Act in eighteenth-century England, rights can change lives for the better and address suffering under authoritarianism.

From Southeast Asian writings and politics of rights studies, I have also learned that the weak and marginalised often understand the workings of authoritarian power and mobilise rights while clear-sighted about its costs and constraints (McCann 2020). To rights mobilisers with pressing needs, critics' anxieties about the potential trappings of a rights hegemony may not pose any primary concern. As Hall, Hirsch and Li (2011) conclude on the paradoxical power of land rights in Indonesia, Thailand, and Vietnam, 'this does not mean . . . that everything is a dilemma for everybody all the time. When farmers are evicted from their land, by force or without compensation, to make way for a dam, there is no dilemma for them' (p. 199). Neither is it a dilemma for Indigenous rights activists, who appreciate the mutability and heterogeneity of their cultures while flying the banner of 'indigeneity' as a means to retain ancestral land and other resources – what truly matters for their lot to thrive (Li 2000; Paredes 2019). Likewise, for sexual and gender minorities activists in Southeast Asia, constructing themselves into a rights-intelligible collective of 'LGBT' is a 'necessary fiction' (Weeks 1995) to forge a stronger opposition against the formidable foes of formal legal orders and social orders of gender and sexuality.

What is moderate at one site or time can be threatening to the established order at another (Marx Ferree 2003). Whether rights are powerful enough to be radically transformative depends on their danger to privileged interests and status favoured and protected by authoritarianism. Rights mobilisation may appear tame in a liberal democracy, a usual means of political participation. However, it may be radical where rights are suppressed or where the recognition of rights undermines deeply rooted norms that sustain social controls and structures of inequality. Hence, Burmese lawyers' insistence on formal procedural rights may seem rather conservative to '[legal] professionals in countries where a reasonable degree of congruence in the basic system of rules can be taken for granted', but it is a radical one within Myanmar (Cheesman and Kyaw Min San 2013, p. 733) – an observation even more poignant in the bloody aftermath of the 2021 military coup that overrode the results of a legally held election.[28]

Notwithstanding their use of existing resources to construct rights practices, mobilisers have produced adaptations to potently threaten the status quo – social, legal and political orders that have benefitted and shielded those at the top. Looking around Southeast Asia, we can find evidence of the unsettling nature of rights to powerful authoritarians that was so profound that it cost life and limb to mobilisers: Thai farmers who rose up in 1973 for their legal rights against landlords and ruling elites were kidnapped, tortured and assassinated, so

---

[28] For analyses of the coup and ongoing violence, see, for example, Charney (2021); Thein-Lemelson (2021).

menacing were their claims to existing hierarchy and mode of economic production (Haberkorn 2011). And, more recently, when a nineteen-year-old in Yangon exercised what she believed were her basic rights to elect her leader and then call upon the results to be honoured, she personified a threat so alarming to the interests of the military that she had to be put down with a bullet to the head.[29]

Conclusion

In this Element, I introduced 'politics of rights' as the entry point to examine rights in Southeast Asia. Rather than emphasise the meanings of rights as they are denoted on statute books, pronounced in court verdicts or theorised abstractedly in philosophical debates, this empirically grounded, socio-legal approach treats rights as social practices whereby rights take on meaning and effects as they are put into action by individual and groups of people. Rights practices constitute the processes of rights mobilisation, the main concept behind politics of rights. The three features of rights mobilisation – decentring law on the books; the interplay between structural and subjective conditions; and plural practices of rights – guide us to investigate the 'how', 'what' and 'why' of rights: how people think, act, feel and behave in relation to their troubles and rights (if any), what happened as a result of their decisions to mobilise rights (or not) and why those events transpired.

Responding to a variety of social controls that lend force to authoritarian structures, mobilisers across Southeast Asia altogether generate a vast repertoire of rights practices. Contingent upon time, place and the people involved, these heterogeneous practices produce uneven, mixed results overall. In some instances, rights mobilisation attained instrumental wins or cultivated cultural changes; in other cases, rights mobilisation turned out to be the opposite, ineffectual and ineffective. This Janus-faced nature of rights, critical scholars argue, is the reason rights can become problematic, seducing people into their relentless pursuit and then leading them to end up with little reward and perhaps with more harm than good.

In the final analysis, I asked that we give rights a chance. Because the theoretical framing of politics of rights enables scholars to be plurally mindful (McCargo 2012) – both of authoritarian power and social controls and of practices and outcomes – it presents us with invaluable opportunities to theorise

---

[29] Mya Thwe Thwe Khaing is believed to be the first person killed by Burmese security forces in the 2021 protests: www.bbc.com/news/world-asia-56005909 (last accessed 28 April 2021). Since her death on 10 February 2021, the violence and number of casualties have escalated: www .hrw.org/asia/myanmar-burma (last accessed 28 November 2021).

more carefully about the capacity of rights to help the dispossessed and disen-franchised. Despite their harsh appraisal of rights, leading TWAIL scholars send a key message that resonates with the core ideas of politics of rights. Instead of fixating on the ills of top-down projects – the primary target of TWAIL criticisms – these scholars find hope in resistance 'from below' and encourage us to attend to how subaltern populations recreate rights from diverse geneal-ogies (Rajagopal 2003). Regardless of rights' imperfections and unfulfilled promises, 'how can the most disadvantaged appropriate and define human rights in what that would make a real difference to their everyday lives?' (Anghie 2013, p. 124).

I would go further in this conclusion. I would embrace the incoherence of rights and take a long view of resistance and mobilisation. Rights practices, in all their mélanges and variations, are likely going to fall short more frequently than they are going to live up to expectations. Nevertheless, the prospects of rights for progressive justice, whether in Southeast Asia or elsewhere, are not and should not be only about the contemporary and immediate. The endeavours of resisters may not easily dissemble morality, economic imperatives or social order, right here, right now. But their creativity and tenacity hold the promise to gradually alter meanings and practices, as they generate the power of rights from the cumulation of material wins and cultural transformations. In a recent essay, I proposed that we think of the temporality of resistance as being in constant interregna (Chua 2021): individuals sometimes labour on their own, other times co-labour with one another, to resist centre stage or off-stage. Episodes of contention and sustained movements are connected to past and future strife, winning, losing or suspending in stalemate as power relations rise and fall. Coercive power may not recede in one episode, one movement or one lifetime. But when we take the longer view, we appreciate the power of rights as diffused across yet vested collectively in individuals and groups, and we find its resilience nurtured through interconnected pasts, presents and futures. We catch glimmers of hope, precedents of victory and models to emulate when we situate rights campaigns for social justice as part of 'ongoing trench battles in larger, sustained historical struggles' (McCann 2020, p. 398).

Along with this longer view, there is a unique place for scholars who study politics of rights in Southeast Asia, especially those of us who work and live in the region. We inhabit, perhaps grew up with, some of the region's contradic-tions and pluralities. We may have felt the layers of authoritarianism, from state institutions to places of worship, even to families of our own flesh and blood. We may have witnessed or experienced more suffering in the absence of rights than in their abundance. Our immersion in Southeast Asia furnishes us with sensitivity to identify oppression of all shapes and magnitude, with acuity to recognise enterprise that chips away at barricades and sanctions and with empathy to understand and live with incoherence. But this kind of faculty may come at a price. Conducting research on politics of rights could discomfort state and non-state authoritarians. To them, researching rights mobilisation might seem like doing rights activism by another name, and scholars who show the humanity and agency of resisters are no different from their research subjects, troublemakers to be banned, channelled away and disciplined. Fellow academics might reject politics of rights scholars for being 'biased' and insinuate accusations of 'indoctrinating' the young and gullible, sometimes without missing a beat from praising scholarship that endorses the status quo and neglects subjectivities by demonstrating 'rationality' and 'objectivity' in their evaluations.

Faced with these unpleasant possibilities, it is easy to feel intimidated and waver about what we have chosen to study. These choices are never easy. I would urge that we hold firmly onto our commitment to the values of politics of rights – with both emic and etic sensitivities, to be fair to the empirical realities that we discover, to give voice to resisters but not overlook their flaws and to empathise with both resisters and anti-resisters while scrutinising the impact of anti-resistance on the power of rights. In solidarity with the bearers and movers of rights in the trenches, with each study we gain incremental advances for rights, too – by tracing suffering, attending to agency and interrogating power. Together, we have to believe that intermittent concessions and eventual breakthroughs are possible, and we give one another succour in the knowledge that any glint of success requires persistent petition and prosecution.

References

Albiston, C. R. (2005). Bargaining in the shadow of social institutions: competing discourses and social change in workplace mobilization of civil rights. *Law and Society Review* 39(1), 11–50.

Amirthalingam, K. (2005). Women's rights, international norms, and domestic violence: Asian perspectives. *Human Rights Quarterly* 27, 683–708.

Anghie, A. (2004). *Imperialism, Sovereignty and the Making of International Law.* New York: Cambridge University Press.

(2013). International human rights law and a developing world perspective. In S. Sheeran and N. Rodley, eds., *Routledge Handbook of International Human Rights Law*, pp. 109–25. Abingdon, UK: Routledge.

Armstrong, E. A., and M. Bernstein (2008). Culture, power, and institutions: a multi-institutional politics approach to social movements. *Sociological Theory* 26(1), 74–99.

Arrington, C. L., and P. Goedde, eds. (2021). *Rights Claiming in South Korea.* New York: Cambridge University Press.

Aspinall, E. (2013). A nation in fragments: patronage and neoliberalism in contemporary Indonesia. *Critical Asian Studies* 45(1), 27–54.

(2019). Conclusion: social movements, patronage democracy, and populist backlash in Indonesia. In T. Dibley and M. Ford, eds., *Activists in Transition: Progressive Politics in Democratic Indonesia*, pp. 187–201. Ithaca, NY: Cornell University Press.

Atsufumi, K., ed. (2016). *Weaving Women's Spheres in Vietnam: The Agency of Women in Family, Religion and Community.* Leiden: Brill.

Bal, C. S. (2015). Dealing with deportability: deportation laws and the political personhood of temporary migrant workers in Singapore. *Asian Journal of Law and Society* 2(2), 267–84.

Bell, D. A. (2000). *East Meets West: Human Rights and Democracy in East Asia.* Princeton, NJ: Princeton University Press.

Bertrand, J. (2011). 'Indigenous peoples' rights' as a strategy of ethnic accommodation: contrasting experiences of Cordillerans and Papuans in the Philippines and Indonesia. *Ethnic and Racial Studies* 34(5), 850–69.

Bourdieu, P. (1977). *Outline of a Theory of Practice*, translated by R. Nice. Cambridge: Cambridge University Press.

Brosius, J. P. (1997). Prior transcripts, divergent paths: resistance and acquiescence to logging in Sarawak, East Malaysia. *Comparative Studies in Society and History* 39(3), 468–510.

(2003). The forest and the nation: negotiating citizenship in Sarawak, East Malaysia. In R. Rosaldo, ed., *Cultural Citizenship in Island Southeast Asia: Nation and Belonging in the Hinterlands*, pp. 76–133. Oakland: University of California Press.

Caouette, D., and S. Turner, eds. (2009). *Agrarian Angst and Rural Resistance in Contemporary Southeast Asia*. Abingdon, UK: Routledge.

Caraway, T. L., and M. Ford (2020). *Labor and Politics in Indonesia*. Cambridge: Cambridge University Press.

Charney, M. W. (2021). Myanmar coup: how the military has held onto power for 60 years. https://theconversation.com/myanmar-coup-how-the-military-has-held-onto-power-for-60-years-154526 (last accessed 24 November 2021).

Cheesman, N. (2015). *Opposing the Rule of Law: How Myanmar's Courts Make Law and Order*. Cambridge: Cambridge University Press.

(2016). Reading Hobbes's sovereign into a Burmese narrative of police torture. *Asia-Pacific Journal on Human Rights and the Law* 17(2), 199–211.

(2017). How in Myanmar 'national races' came to surpass citizenship and exclude Rohingya. *Journal of Contemporary Asia* 47(3), 461–83.

(2021). State terror and torture: the hatred of politics in Myanmar. www.abc.net.au/religion/state-terror-torture-and-anti-politics-in-myanmar/13270932 (last visited 29 April 2021)

Cheesman, N., and Kyaw Min San (2013). Not just defending: advocating for law in Myanmar. *Wisconsin International Law Journal* 31, 702–33.

Christensen, S. R., and A. Rabibhadana (1994). Exit, voice, and the depletion of open access resources: the political bases of property rights in Thailand. *Law & Society Review* 28(3), 639–56.

Chua, L. J. (2014). *Mobilizing Gay Singapore: Rights and Resistance in an Authoritarian State*. Philadelphia, PA: Temple University Press.

(2015). The vernacular mobilization of human rights in Myanmar's sexual orientation and gender identity movement. *Law & Society Review* 49(2), 299–332.

(2016). Negotiating social norms and relations in the micromobilization of human rights: the case of Burmese lesbian activism. *Law and Social Inquiry* 41(3), 643–69.

(2017). Collective litigation and the constitutional challenges to decriminalizing homosexuality in Singapore. *Journal of Law and Society* 44(3), 433–55.

(2019a). *The Politics of Love in Myanmar: LGBT Mobilization and Human Rights as a Way of Life*. Stanford, CA: Stanford University Press.

(2019b). Legal mobilization and authoritarianism. *Annual Review of Law and Social Science* 15(1), 355–76.

(2021). Interregna: Time, law and resistance. *Law and Social Inquiry* 46(1): 268–91.

Chua, L. J., and D. Gilbert (2015). Sexual orientation and gender minorities in transition: LGBT rights and activism in Myanmar. *Human Rights Quarterly* 37(1), 1–28.

Chua, L. J., and T. Hildebrandt (2014). From health crisis to gay advocacy? HIV-AIDS and gay rights activism in China and Singapore. *Voluntas: International Journal of Voluntary and Nonprofit Organizations* 25(6), 1583–1605.

Collier, J., D. Engel and B. Yngvesson (1994). Editors' introduction. *Law and Society Review* 28(3), 417–28.

Cornwall, A., and M. Molyneux, eds. (2008). *The Politics of Rights: Dilemmas for Feminist Praxis*. New York: Routledge.

Coulibaly, M., P. Claeys and A. Berson (2020). The right to seeds and legal mobilization for the protection of peasant seed systems in Mali. *Journal of Human Rights Practice* 12(3), 479–500.

Crouch, M. (2013). Asian legal transplants and rule of law reform: national human rights commission in Myanmar and Indonesia. *Hague Journal on the Rule of Law* 5, 146–77.

Curley, M. (2018). Governing civil society in Cambodia: implications of the NGO law for the 'Rule of Law'. *Asian Studies Review* 42(2), 247–67.

Curnow, J. (2015). Legal support structures and the realisation of Muslim women's rights in Indonesia. *Asian Studies Review* 39(2), 213–28.

Dale, J. G. (2011). *Free Burma: Transnational Legal Action and Corporate Accountability*. Minneapolis: University of Minnesota Press.

Dibley, T. (2019). Democratization and disability activism in Indonesia. In T. Dibley and M. Ford, eds., *Activists in Transition: Progressive Politics in Democratic Indonesia*, pp. 171–86. Ithaca, NY: Cornell University Press.

Digeser, P. (1992). The fourth face of power. *Journal of Politics* 54(4), 977–1007.

Diprose, G., and A. McGregor (2009). Dissolving the sugar fields: land reform and resistance identities in the Philippines. *Singapore Journal of Tropical Geography* 30, 52–69.

Dressler, W. H. (2009). Resisting local inequities: community-based conservation on Palawan Island, the Philippines. In D. Caouette and S. Turner, eds., *Agrarian Angst and Rural Resistance in Contemporary Southeast Asia*, pp. 82–104. London: Routledge.

Dudas, J. R. (2008). *The Cultivation of Resentment: Treaty Rights and the New Right*. Stanford, CA: Stanford University Press.

Duxbury, A., and H.-L. Tan (2019). *Can ASEAN Take Human Rights Seriously?* Cambridge: Cambridge University Press.

Earl, J. (2011). Political repression: iron fists, velvet gloves, and diffuse control. *Annual Review of Sociology* 37, 261–84.

Ela, N. (2017). Litigation dilemmas: lessons from the Marcos human rights class action. *Law & Social Inquiry* 42(2), 479–508.

Eldridge, P. J. (2002). *The Politics of Human Rights in Southeast Asia*. London: Routledge.

Engel, D. M. (2012). Vertical and horizontal perspectives on rights consciousness. *Indiana Journal of Global Legal Studies* 19(2), 423–55.

(2016). Blood curse and belonging in Thailand: law, Buddhism, and legal consciousness. *Asian Journal of Law and Society* 3(1), 71–83.

Engel, D. M., and Engel, J. S. (2010). *Tort, Custom, and Karma: Globalization and Legal Consciousness in Thailand*. Stanford, CA: Stanford University Press.

Encarnación, O. G. (2016). *Out in the Periphery: Latin America's Gay Rights Revolution*. New York: Oxford University Press.

Fealy, G. (2019). Reformasi and the decline of liberal Islam. In T. Dibley and M. Ford, eds., *Activists in Transition: Progressive Politics in Democratic Indonesia*, pp. 117–34. Ithaca, NY: Cornell University Press.

Fletcher, R. (2007). Introduction: beyond resistance? In R. Fletcher, ed., *Beyond Resistance: The Future of Freedom*, pp. vii–xxv. Hauppauge, NY: Nova Science Publishers .

Fligstein, N., and McAdam, D. (2011). Toward a general theory of strategic action fields. *Sociological Theory* 29(1), 1–26.

Ford, N., Wilson, D., Cawthorne, P., Kumphitak, A., Kasi-Sedapan, S., Kaetkaew, S., Teemanka, S., Donmon, B., and Preuanbuapan, C. (2009). Challenge and co-operation: civil society activism for access to HIV treatment in Thailand. *Tropical Medicine and International Health* 14(3), 258–66.

Foucault, M. (1979). *Discipline and Punish: The Birth of the Prison*. New York: Vintage Books.

Fraenkel, E. (1941). *The Dual State: A Contribution to the Theory of Dictatorship*. Oxford: Oxford University Press.

Fraser, Nancy. (1995). From redistribution to recognition? Dilemmas of justice in a 'postsocialist' age. *New Left Review* 212: 68–93.

Freeman, C. (2010). Introduction. In A. Ong, *Spirits of Resistance and Capitalist Discipline: Factory Women in Malaysia*, 2nd ed., pp. xv–xx. Albany: State University of New York Press.

Gaventa, J. (1982). *Power and Powerlessness: Quiescence and Rebellion in an Appalachian Valley*. Urbana: University of Illinois Press.

Gidley, R. (2019). *Illiberal Transitional Justice and the Extraordinary Chambers in the Courts of Cambodia*. London: Palgrave.

Gillespie, J. (2018). The role of emotion in land regulation: an empirical study of online advocacy in authoritarian Asia. *Law and Society Review* 52(1), 106–39.

Gillespie, J., and Nguyen, Q. H. (2019). Between authoritarian governance and urban citizenship: tree-felling protests in Hanoi. *Urban Studies* 56(5), 977–91.

Goh, J. N., and Kananatu, T. (2019). *Mak nyahs* and the dismantling of dehumanisation: framing empowerment strategies of Malaysian male-to-female transsexuals in the 2000s. *Sexualities* 22(1–2), 114–30.

Golder, B. (2015). *Foucault and the Politics of Rights*. Stanford, CA: Stanford University Press.

Gomez, J., and Ramcharan, R. (eds.) (2020). *National Human Rights Institutions in Southeast Asia: Selected Case Studies*. Singapore: Palgrave Macmillan.

Goodale, M. (2007). The power of right(s): tracking empires of law and new modes of social resistance in Bolivia (and elsewhere). In M. Goodale and S. E. Merry, eds., *The Practice of Human Rights: Tracking Law between the Global and the Local*, pp. 130–62. New York: Cambridge University Press.

Gorman, T. (2014). Moral economy and the upper peasant: the dynamics of land privatization in the Mekong Delta. *Journal of Agrarian Change* 14(4), 501–21.

Gramsci, A. (1971). *Selections from the Prison Notebooks*. New York: International Publishers.

Grenfell, L. (2015). Realising rights in Timor-Leste. *Asian Studies Review* 39(2), 266–83.

Haberkorn, T. (2011). *Revolution Interrupted: Farmers, Students, Law, and Violence in Northern Thailand*. Madison: University of Wisconsin Press.

Haberkorn, T. (2018). *In Plain Sight: Impunity and Human Rights in Thailand*. Madison: University of Wisconsin Press.

Hall, D., Hirsch, P., and Li, T. (2011). *Powers of Exclusion: Land Dilemmas in Southeast Asia*, Singapore: NUS Press.

Hamid, A. F. A. (2016). Syariahization of intra-Muslim religious freedom and human rights practice in Malaysia: the case of Darul Arqam. *Contemporary Southeast Asia* 38(1), 28–54.

Harms, E. (2016). *Luxury and Rubble: Civility and Dispossession in the New Saigon.* Oakland: University of California Press.

Harriden, J. (2012). *The Authority of Influence: Women and Power in Burmese History.* Copenhagen: NIAS Press.

Hayward, S., and Frydenlund, I. (2019). Religion, secularism, and the pursuit of peace in Myanmar. *Review of Faith & International Affairs* 17(4), 1–11.

Ho, E. L.-E., and Chua, L. J. (2016). Law and 'race' in the citizenship spaces of Myanmar: spatial strategies and the political subjectivity of the Burmese Chinese. *Ethnic and Racial Studies* 39(5), 896–916.

Holden, W. N. (2005). Civil society opposition to nonferrous metals mining in the Philippines. *Voluntas: International Journal of Voluntary and Nonprofit Organizations* 16(3), 223–49.

Hollander, J. A., and Einwohner, R. L. (2004). Conceptualizing resistance. *Sociological Forum* 19(4): 533–54.

Holzmeyer, C. (2009). Human rights in an era of neoliberal globalization: the Alien Tort Claims Act and grassroots mobilization in *Doe v. Unocal. Law and Society Review* 43(2), 271–304.

Ibrahim, N. A. (2018). Everyday authoritarianism: a political anthropology of Singapore. *Critical Asian Studies* 50(2), 219–31.

Irianto, S. (2004). Competition and interaction between state law and customary law in the court room: a study of inheritance cases in Indonesia. *Journal of Legal Pluralism and Unofficial Law* 36(49), 91–112.

Jeffrey, R. (2016). Trading amnesty for impunity in Timor-Leste. *Conflict, Security and Development* 16(1), 33–51.

Kananatu, T. (2020). *Minorities, Rights and the Law in Malaysia.* New York: Routledge.

Keeler, W. (2017). *The Traffic in Hierarchy: Masculinity and Its Others in Buddhist Burma.* Honolulu: University of Hawaii Press.

Kemp, A., and Kfir, N. (2016). Mobilizing migrant workers' rights in 'non-immigration' countries: the politics of resonance and migrants' rights activism in Israel and Singapore. *Law and Society Review* 50(1), 82–116.

Kent, A. (2011). Global change and moral uncertainty: why do Cambodian women seek refuge in Buddhism? *Global Change, Peace and Security* 23(3), 405–19.

Kerkvliet, B. J. T. (2005). *The Power of Everyday Politics: How Vietnamese Peasants Transformed National Policy.* Ithaca, NY: Cornell University Press.

(2009). Everyday politics in peasant societies (and ours). *Journal of Peasant Studies* 36(1), 227–43.

(2014). Protests over land in Vietnam: rightful resistance and more. *Journal of Vietnamese Studies* 9(3), 19–54.

Kessler, M. (1990). Legal mobilization for social reform: power and the politics of agenda setting. *Law and Society Review* 24(1), 121–43.

Kuhonta, E. M. (2009). Development and its discontents: the case of the Pak Mun Dam in northeastern Thailand. In D. Caouette and S. Turner, eds., *Agrarian Angst and Rural Resistance in Contemporary Southeast Asia*, pp. 135–58. London: Routledge.

Lehoucq, E. (2021). Legal threats and the emergence of legal mobilization: conservative mobilization in Colombia. *Law & Social Inquiry* 46(2), 299–330.

Lev, D. S. (2000). Judicial institutions and legal culture. In D. S. Lev, *Legal Evolution and Political Authority in Indonesia: Selected Essays*, pp. 161–214. Boston, MA: Kluwer Law International.

Levitsky, S. R. (2014). *Caring for Our Own: Why There Is No Political Demand for New American Social Welfare Rights*. New York: Oxford University Press.

Merry, S. E. 2006. *Human Rights and Gender Violence: Translating International Law into Local Justice*. Chicago, IL: University of Chicago Press.

Li, T. M. (2000). Articulating indigenous identity in Indonesia: resource politics and the tribal slot. *Comparative Studies in Society and History* 42(1), 149–79.

Linarelli, J., Salomon, M. E., and Sornarajah, M. (2018). *The Misery of International Law: Confrontations with Injustice in the Global Economy*. Oxford: Oxford University Press.

Liu, S. (2015). Law's social forms: a powerless approach to the sociology of law. *Law and Social Inquiry* 40(1), 1–28.

Lukes, S. (1974). *Power: A Radical View*. New York: Palgrave Macmillan.

Lyons, L. T. (2005). Transient Workers Count Too? The Intersection of Citizenship and Gender in Singapore's Civil Society. *Sojourn* 20(2), 208–48.

Malseed, K. (2008). Where there is no movement: local resistance and the potential for solidarity. *Journal of Agrarian Change* 8(2 and 3), 489–514.

Manning, P. (2017). *Transitional Justice and Memory in Cambodia: Beyond the Extraordinary Chambers*. New York: Routledge.

Mansbridge, J. J., and Morris, A. (eds.) (2001). *Oppositional Consciousness: The Subjective Roots of Social Protest*. Chicago, IL: University of Chicago Press.

Massad, J. A. (2002). Re-orienting desire: the Gay International and the Arab World. *Public Culture* 14(2), 361–85.

Mark, S. (2016). Are the odds of justice 'stacked' against them? Challenges and opportunities for securing land claims by smallholder farmers in Myanmar. *Critical Asian Studies* 48(3), 443–60.

Marx Ferree, M. (2003). Resonance and radicalism: feminist framing in the abortion debates of the United States and Germany. *American Journal of Sociology* 109(2), 304–44.

McAdam, D. (1999). Introduction to the Second Edition. In *Political Process and the Development of Black Insurgency, 1930–1950*, 2nd ed., pp. vii–xlii. Chicago, IL: University of Chicago Press.

McCann, M. W. (1994). *Rights at Work: Pay Equity Reform and the Politics of Legal Mobilization*. Chicago, IL: University of Chicago Press.

(2014). The unbearable lightness of rights: on sociolegal inquiry in the global era. *Law and Society Review* 48(2), 245–73.

McCann, M. W. (with Lovell, G. I.) (2020). *Union by Law: Filipino American Labor Activists, Rights Radicalism, and Racial Capitalism*. Chicago, IL: University of Chicago Press.

McCargo, D. (2012). Against wishful scholarship: the importance of Engel. *Indiana Journal of Global Legal Studies* 19(2), 489–93.

McConnachie, K. (2014). *Governing Refugees: Justice, Order and Legal Pluralism*. New York: Routledge.

McAllister, K. E. (2015). Rubber, rights and resistance: the evolution of local struggles against a Chinese rubber concession in Northern Laos. *Journal of Peasant Studies* 42(3–4), 817–37.

Minter, T., Ploeg, J., Pedrablanca, M., Sunderland, T., and Persoon, G. (2014). Limits to indigenous participation: the Agta and the Northern Sierra Madre Natural Park, the Philippines. *Human Ecology* 42, 769–78.

Mohan, M. (2013). The road to Song Mao: transnational litigation from Southeast Asia to the United Kingdom. *American Journal of International Law* 107(4), 30–36.

Morreira, S. (2016). *Rights After Wrongs: Local Knowledge and Human Rights in Zimbabwe*. Stanford, CA: Stanford University Press.

Moustafa, T. (2018). *Constituting Religion: Islam, Liberal Rights and the Malaysian State*. New York: Cambridge University Press.

Mostowlansky, T., and Rota, A. (2020). Emic and etic. In F. Stein, S. Lazar, M. Candea, H. Diemberger, J. Robbins, A. Sanchez and R. Stasch, eds.,

The Cambridge Encyclopedia of Anthropology. DOI: http://doi.org/10 .29164/20emicetic.

Muller, D. M. (2015). Sharia law and the politics of 'faith control' in Brunei Darussalam: dynamics of socio-legal change in a Southeast Asian sultanate. *Internationales Asienforum* 46(3–4), 313–45.

Munger, F. W. (2006). Culture, power, and law: thinking about the anthropology of rights in Thailand in an era of globalization. *New York Law School Law Review* 51, 817–38.

   (2014). Revolution imagined: cause advocacy, consumer rights, and the evolving role of NGOs in Thailand. *Asian Journal of Comparative Law* 9(1), 29–64.

Nader, L. (2001). Harmony coerced is freedom denied. www.chronicle.com /article/harmony-coerced-is-freedom-denied/ (last accessed 6 March 2021).

Neo, J. (2012). Incorporating human rights: mitigated dualism and interpretation in Malaysian Courts. *Asian Yearbook of International Law* 18, 1–37.

Nguyen, T. P. (2018). Labour law and (in)justice in workers' letters in Vietnam. *Asian Journal of Law & Society* 5(1), 25–47.

   (2019). *Workplace Justice: Rights and Labour Resistance in Vietnam*. Singapore: Palgrave Macmillan.

Nonet, P., and Selznick, P. (1978). *Law and Society in Transition: Toward Responsive Law*. New York: Harper & Row.

O'Brien, K., and Li, L. (2006). *Rightful Resistance in Rural China*. New York: Cambridge University Press.

Olivius, E., and Hedström, J. (2019). Militarized nationalism as a platform for feminist mobilization? The case of the exiled Burmese women's movement. *Women's Studies International Forum*, 76, DOI: 10.1016/j. wsif.2019.102263.

Ong, A. (2010). *Spirits of Resistance and Capitalist Discipline*, 2nd ed. Albany: State University of New York Press.

Ortner, S. B. (2008). *Anthropology and Social Theory: Culture, Power, and the Acting Subject*. Durham, NC: Duke University Press.

Park, C. M. Y. (2018). 'Our lands are our lives': gendered experiences of resistance to land grabbing in rural Cambodia. *Feminist Economics* 25(4), 1–24.

Peluso, N. L. (2003). Territorializing local struggles for resource control: a look at environmental discourses and politics in Indonesia. In P. Greenough and A. L. Tsing, eds., *Nature in the Global South: Environmental Projects in*

South and Southeast Asia, pp. 231–52. Durham, NC: Duke University Press.

Paredes, O. (2019). Preserving 'tradition': the business of indigeneity in the modern Philippine context. *Journal of Southeast Asian Studies* 50(1), 86–106.

Prasse-Freeman, E. (2016). Grassroots protest movements and mutating conceptions of 'the political' in an evolving Burma. In R. Egreteau and F. Robinne, eds., *Metamorphosis: Studies in Social and Political Change in Myanmar*, pp. 69–100. Singapore: NUS Press.

(2020). Resistance/refusal: politics of manoeuvre under diffuse regimes of governmentality. *Anthropological Theory* 0(0), 1–26.

Puar, J. K. (2002). Circuits of queer mobility: tourism, travel, and globalization. *GLQ: A Journal of Lesbian and Gay Studies* 8(1), 101–37.

Rajah, J. (2012) *Authoritarian Rule of Law: Legislation, Discourse and Legitimacy in Singapore*. Cambridge: Cambridge University Press.

Rajagopal, B. (2003). *International Law from Below: Development, Social Movements and Third World Resistance*. Cambridge: Cambridge University Press.

Revillard, A. (2017). Social movements and the politics of bureaucratic rights enforcement: insights from the allocation of disability rights in France. *Law & Social Inquiry*, 42(2),450–478.

Reynolds, F. E. (1994). Dhamma in dispute: the interactions of religion and law in Thailand. *Law and Society Review* 28(3), 433–52.

Rodan, G. (2003). Embracing electronic media but suppressing civil society: authoritarian consolidation in Singapore. *Pacific Review* 16(4), 503–24.

Rosser, A. (2015). Law and the realization of human rights: insights from Indonesia's education sector. *Asian Studies Review* 39(2), 194–212.

Schattschneider, E. E. (1975). *The Semi-Sovereign People: A Realist's View of Democracy in America*. Hinsdale, IL: Dryden Press.

Scheingold, S. (2004). *The Politics of Rights: Lawyers, Public Policy, and Political Change*, 2nd ed. Ann Arbor: University of Michigan Press.

Scott, J. C. (1984). *Weapons of the Weak: Everyday Forms of Peasant Resistance*. New Haven, CT: Yale University Press.

(1990). *Domination and the Arts of Resistance: Hidden Transcripts*. New Haven, CT: Yale University Press.

(2009). *The Art of Not Being Governed: An Anarchist History of Upland Southeast Asia*. New Haven, CT: Yale University Press.

Selby, D. (2018) *Human rights in Thailand*. Philadelphia: University of Pennsylvania Press.

Sewell, W. H., Jr. (1992). A theory of structure: duality, agency, and transformation. *American Journal of Sociology* 98(1), 1–29.

Shirley, R. G., and Word, J. (2018). Rights, rivers and renewables: lessons from hydropower conflict in Borneo on the role of cultural politics in energy planning for Small Island Developing States. *Utilities Policy* 55, 189–99.

Silliman, G. S. (1981–2). Dispute processing by the Philippine agrarian court. *Law and Society Review* 16(1), 89–114.

Sims, K. (2020) Risk navigation for thinking and working politically: the work and disappearance of Sombath Somphone. *Development Policy Review*, DOI: https://doi.org/10.1111/dpr.12527.

Smith, R. M. (1997). *Civic Ideals: Conflicting Visions of Citizenship in US History*. New Haven, CT: Yale University Press.

Speed, S. (2008). *Rights in Rebellion Indigenous Struggle and Human Rights in Chiapas*. Stanford, CA: Stanford University Press.

Swidler, A. (1986). Culture in action: symbols and strategies. *American Sociological Review* 51(2), 273–86.

Tan, H.-L. (2011). *The ASEAN Intergovernmental Commission on Human Rights: Institutionalising Human Rights in Southeast Asia*. Cambridge: Cambridge University Press.

Taylor, P. (2014) Coercive localization in Southwest Vietnam: Khmer land disputes and the containment of dissent. *Journal of Vietnamese Studies* 9 (3), 55–90.

Thein-Lemelson, S. M. (2021). 'Politicide' and the Myanmar coup. *Anthropology Today* 37(2), 3–5.

Theriault, N. (2011). The micropolitics of indigenous environmental movements in the Philippines. *Development and Change* 42(6), 1417–40.

Thompson, E. P. (1975). *Whigs and Hunters: The Origin of the Black Act*. New York: Pantheon Books.

Thoreson, R. R. (2012). Realizing rights in Manila: brokers and the mediation of sexual politics in the Philippines. *GLQ: A Journal of Lesbian and Gay Studies* 18(4), 529–63.

Tilly, C., and S. Tarrow. (2007). *Contentious Politics*. London: Paradigm Publishers.

Turner, S., and Michaud, J. (2009). 'Weapons of the week': Selective resistance and agency among the Hmong in northern Vietnam. In D. Caouette and S. Turner, eds., *Agrarian Angst and Rural Resistance in Contemporary Southeast Asia*, pp. 45–60. London: Routledge.

Van der Vet, F. (2018). 'When they come for you': legal mobilization in new authoritarian Russia. *Law and Society Review* 52(2), 301–36.

Varol, O. O. (2015). Stealth authoritarianism. *Iowa Law Review* 100, 1673–1742.

Walton, M. J., McKay, M. and Daw Khin Mar Mar Kyi (2015). Women and Myanmar's 'Religious Protection Laws'. *Review of Faith & International Affairs* 13(4), 36–49.

Wang, D., and Liu, S. (2020). Performing artivism: feminists, lawyers, and online legal mobilization in China. *Law and Social Inquiry* 45(3), 678–705.

Weiss, M. L. (2011). *Student Activism in Malaysia: Crucible, Mirror, Sideshow.* Singapore: NUS Press.

(2012). *Politics in Cyberspace: New Media in Malaysia.* Berlin: fesmedia Asia.

(2014). New media, new activism: trends and trajectories in Malaysia, Singapore and Indonesia. *International Development Planning Review* 36(1), 91–109.

Weiss, M., and Hassan, S., eds. (2003). *Social Movements in Malaysia: From Moral Communities to NGOs.* London: Routledge.

Weeks, J. (1995). Necessary fictions: sexual identities and the politics of diversity. In J. Weeks, *Invented Moralities: Sexual Values in an Age of Uncertainty*, pp. 82–101. New York: Columbia University Press.

Yew, W. L. (2016). Constraint without coercion: indirect repression of environmental protest in Malaysia. *Pacific Affairs* 89(3), 543–65.

Young, I. M. (1997). Unruly categories: a critique of Nancy Fraser's dual systems theory. *New Left Review* 222, 147–60.

Zerner, C. (1994). Through a green lens: the construction of customary environmental law and community in Indonesia's Maluku Islands. *Law and Society Review* 28(5), 1079–1122.

Zerner, C. (2003). Sounding the Makassar Strait: the poetics and politics of an Indonesian marine environment. In C. Zerner, ed., *Culture and the Question of Rights: Forests, Coasts, and Seas in Southeast Asia*, pp. 56–108. London: Duke University Press.

Zivi, K. (2005). Feminism and the politics of rights: a qualified defense of identity-based rights claiming. *Politics & Gender* 1(3), 377–97.

Acknowledgements

I am grateful to NUS Law's Centre for Asian Legal Studies for providing the research funds and hosting a manuscript workshop for this project in March 2021; to Tony Anghie, Michael McCann and the workshop attendees for their feedback; to series editors Edward Aspinall and Meredith Weiss for their belief in this project; to Umika Sharma, Wen Weiyang, Xie Yihui and Jeanette Yeo for their research assistance; and to David Engel, Jaruwan Engel, Mark Goodale and Andrew Simester for their support and encouragement.

Cambridge Elements ≡

Politics and Society in Southeast Asia

Edward Aspinall

Australian National University

Edward Aspinall is a professor of politics at the Coral Bell School of Asia-Pacific Affairs, Australian National University. A specialist of Southeast Asia, especially Indonesia, much of his research has focused on democratisation, ethnic politics and civil society in Indonesia and, most recently, clientelism across Southeast Asia.

Meredith L. Weiss

University at Albany, SUNY

Meredith L. Weiss is Professor of Political Science at the University at Albany, SUNY. Her research addresses political mobilization and contention, the politics of identity and development, and electoral politics in Southeast Asia, with particular focus on Malaysia and Singapore.

About the series

The Elements series Politics and Society in Southeast Asia includes both country-specific and thematic studies on one of the world's most dynamic regions. Each title, written by a leading scholar of that country or theme, combines a succinct, comprehensive, up-to-date overview of debates in the scholarly literature with original analysis and a clear argument.

Cambridge Elements $\equiv$

Politics and Society in Southeast Asia

Elements in the series

Indonesia: Twenty Years after Democracy
Jamie Davidson

Civil–Military Relations in Southeast Asia
Aurel Croissant

Singapore: Identity, Brand, Power
Kenneth Paul Tan

Ritual and Region: The Invention of ASEAN
Mathew Davies

Populism in Southeast Asia
Paul Kenny

Cambodia: Return to Authoritarianism
Kheang Un

Vietnam: A Pathway from State Socialism
Thaveeporn Vasavakul

Independent Timor-Leste: Regime, Economy and Identity
Douglas Kammen

Media and Power in Southeast Asia
Cherian George and Gayathry Venkiteswaran

The Rise of Sophisticated Authoritarianism in Southeast Asia
Lee Morgenbesser

Rural Development in Southeast Asia
Jonathan Rigg

Fighting Armed Conflicts in Southeast Asia
Shane Joshua Barter

Democratic Deconsolidation in Southeast Asia
Marcus Mietzner

Gender in Southeast Asia
Mina Roces

Ethnicity and Politics in Southeast Asia
Amy H. Liu and Jacob I. Ricks

The Politics of Rights and Southeast Asia
Lynette J. Chua

A full series listing is available at: www.cambridge.org/ESEA

Printed in the United States
by Baker & Taylor Publisher Services